W9-CEB-197

73601

PRINCES OF WALES

PRINCES OF WALES

By

L. G. PINE

CHARLES E. TUTTLE CO.: PUBLISHERS
Rutland, Vermont

Representatives
Continental Europe: BOXERBOOKS, INC., *Zurich*
Canada: M. G. HURTIG LTD., *Edmonton*

Published by the Charles E. Tuttle Company, Inc.
of Rutland, Vermont & Tokyo, Japan
with editorial offices at
Suido 1-chome, 2-6, Bunkyo-ku, Tokyo, Japan

© *1970 by Charles E. Tuttle Co., Inc.*

Library of Congress Catalog Card No. 72-104216

Standard Book No. 8048 0896-1

First edition, 1970

PRINTED IN JAPAN

Contents

List of Illustrations

7

Acknowledgments

The author wishes to acknowledge the courtesy and help of Commander Richard Colville, C.V.O., D.S.C., R.N., Press Secretary, Buckingham Palace; the suggestions for the subject of this book by Mr. Ralph Rolls; and the kindness of Major-General E. A. E. Tremlett, C.B.E., T.D., and of Mr. Douglas Hooke in reading the proofs.

Acknowledgment is also made to Messrs. Butterworth & Co., Ltd., for the extract from Halsbury's *Laws of England*, quoted on pages 178 and 179 of this book.

Preface

I welcome the opportunity opened to me by Mr. Charles Tuttle to bring out a reprint of this work with an additional chapter on the present Prince of Wales. It was unfortunate that the book had gone out of print at the time of the investiture on 1st July 1969, as it was being used and referred to, at that time, as the only work dealing with the history of all the Princes of Wales. However, in the order of nature, Prince Charles will remain Prince of Wales for many years to come and as the various stages of his career are reached, the work will serve its original purpose as a book of reference.

Since the present issue is a reprint save for the last chapter, two or three items need to be adjusted here. Commander Colville (page 8) is now Sir Richard Colville; Dr. Hugh Dalton (page 163) was later created a life peer, as Lord Dalton in 1960. On page 91, my sense of dramatic irony should have a correction as to fact. Richard III was the last king of the Plantagenet family, but not the last descendant of William the Conqueror to reign, since Henry VII descended from him through female lines. Still it is a fact that the great continental dynasty of Norman and Plantagenet sovereigns ended, as it had begun on the battlefield. My meaning in the passages on pages 89–91 is that the native Old English dynasty was terminated in 1066; the artificial connection with France began; it closed with Richard III's death in 1485, and again a native dynasty reigned, under whose sway the English genius once more found its natural development away from Europe.

I wish to thank Squadron Leader David Checketts, Equerry to H.R.H. the Prince of Wales, for reading the proofs of chapter XIII.

Leslie G. Pine

9

CHAPTER I

Introduction

IT was 13th July 1911. The ancient Castle of Caernarvon had, as it were, awakened from the sleep and disuse of centuries. Huge crowds stood around it, or were gathered in orderly and serried ranks within it. All the spectators were filled with anticipation of a brilliant and moving ceremony. For the first time for centuries a Prince of Wales was to be invested and presented to the people of Wales in Caernarvon Castle. His Royal Highness Prince Edward Albert Christian George Andrew Patrick David, eldest son of His Majesty King George V, who had been created by letters-patent 23rd June 1910 as Prince of Wales and Earl of Chester, was now to be invested and proclaimed Prince of the Welsh people in the very surroundings where history, or at least historic legend, stated that the first English Prince of Wales had been presented to the Welsh.

How had this ceremony come to be prepared? It was very largely the fruit of the inspiration of a radical reformer. Mr. (later Earl) Lloyd George was the Chancellor of the Exchequer. His speeches in recent elections had alarmed and distressed many who believed with all their hearts that in the country's old traditions lay the secret of its greatness. But this radical politician was also a Welshman, deeply versed in the lore of his country. He did not claim to speak for Welshmen without knowing how to speak their language. He loved the hills and the history, the scenery and the poetry of Wales. He proposed that the new Prince of Wales should be the centre of a brilliant ceremony, and the new king, George V, readily agreed. Mr. Lloyd George was M.P. for Caernarvon and Constable of Caernarvon Castle. The great day of the prince's presentation would cover him with glory also. He taught his prince to speak words in the ancient Welsh tongue, so that he would reign for ever in Welsh hearts.

So it happened that within the year in which he had succeeded his father on the throne, King George V went to Caernarvon to invest his son and destined successor. No efforts had been spared to make the scene memorable and beautiful. The castle itself is a sufficiently impressive setting for great events. It commemorated by its very existence the history of the great Edward the First (i.e. of the Plantagenet dynasty), who had conceived the idea of making the three countries—England, Wales and Scotland—into one realm. Here was Edward's successor, the sovereign of a united Britain, of an Ireland still united, and of an empire whose extent and power would have been inconceivable to the theorists of the thirteenth century. This sovereign, the Defender of the Faith, the King Emperor, the acknowledged, undisputed head of at least 450 millions of folk of all colours, was surrounded with all the pomp of his armed forces and of his great officers of state. The twentieth Prince of Wales was come for his investiture and was to arrive at the castle about half an hour before the arrival of Their Majesties.

The interior of the castle was arranged amphitheatre-wise, with tiers of seats to hold some ten thousand persons, some being within the Inner and Outer Bailey, and others within the stands in the moat. Apart altogether from these privileged spectators within the castle enclave, an immense multitude had gathered without the walls, and filled the streets of the ancient borough to overflowing capacity. Naturally the greatest concourse of spectators was to be found where a newly erected balcony on the castle overlooked the Castle Square and Slate Quay. Here an act of patriotic generosity by Mr. Assheton-Smith had given many spectators more opportunity of viewing the presentation which was to take place on this balcony. Mr. Assheton-Smith had arranged for certain old houses to be pulled down to clear the view.

When the Prince of Wales arrived at the Castle Square he received an address of welcome from the Mayor and Town Clerk of Caernarvon. It was in his speech of reply that the prince used some of the sentences taught him by Lloyd George. *Mor o gan yw Cymru i gyd*—All Wales is a sea of song; and *Diolch o waelod fy nghalon i hen wlad fy nhadau*—Thanks from the bottom of my heart to the old land of my fathers.

The prince entered the castle and went to the apartments prepared for him, while his standard was run up on the Eagle Tower. Hitherto he had been clad in the uniform of a midshipman, but now he donned the garments appropriate to his new status. There is a curious contrast between the official account of the prince's dress and his own remarks in his memoirs. "A fantastic costume," he says, "designed for the occasion, consisting of white satin breeches and a mantle and surcoat of purple velvet edged with ermine." The official narrative runs: "The dress worn by His Royal Highness as he proceeded from the Chamberlain's Tower to the royal dais consisted of white satin breeches, white silk stockings, black shoes with plain rectangular gold buckles, and a purple velvet surcoat, edged with ermine, slashed with black fur, and with an outer edging of embroidery in mixed dull and bright gold, following the Prince of Wales's plume in design. It was girt at the waist with a purple silk sash, which had cords fringed with purple and gold." It does not require much imagination to understand the reluctance of a midshipman of seventeen to don these elaborate clothes. Still, they had been worn by his many predecessors, and tradition required him to obey precedent.

The approach of the sovereigns themselves was marked with great ceremony. With right royal favour the king knighted the Mayor of Caernarvon and the Sheriff of the County on his approach to the castle, after receiving their loyal addresses. Then when they reached the castle they were presented with the Key to the castle by its chatelain, Mr. Lloyd George. Within the castle was the royal dais, and to this the king and queen proceeded with their magnificent procession. The Royal Standard had been run up in place of that of the Prince of Wales in the Eagle Tower. The prince now advanced, with bare head and wearing his surcoat and knee breeches, to the dais. He then knelt upon a cushion before the king, his father. The Home Secretary, Mr. Winston Churchill, read the letters patent. As they were read the king, at the appropriate points, carried out the ceremony of investiture.

"George the Fifth by the Grace of God of the United Kingdom of Great Britain and Ireland and of the British Dominions beyond the Seas, King, Defender of the Faith—To all Archbishops, Dukes, Marquesses, Earls, Viscounts, Bishops, Barons, Baronets, Knights, Justices, Provosts, Ministers and all Our faithful Subjects Greeting—Know ye that We have made and created other and by these our Letters Patent do make and create [at this point the king invested the prince with the Mantle] Our Most Dear Son, Edward Albert Christian George Andrew Patrick David, Prince of the United Kingdom of Great Britain and Ireland, Duke of Cornwall and Rothesay, Earl of Carrick, Baron of Renfrew, Lord of the Isles, and Great Steward of Scotland, Duke of Saxony and Prince of Saxe-Cobourg and Gotha, PRINCE OF WALES AND EARL OF CHESTER, and to the same Our Most Dear Son Edward Albert Christian George Andrew Patrick David have given and granted And by this Our present Charter do give grant and confirm the Name, Style, Title, Dignity, and Honour of the same Principality and Earldom, And Him Our said Most Dear Son Edward Albert Christian George Andrew Patrick David, as has been accustomed, We do Ennoble and Invest with the said Principality and Earldom by Girding Him with a Sword [here the king invested the prince with the sword by hanging it round his neck], By putting a Coronet on His Head [here the king placed the Coronet upon the prince's head], And a Gold Ring on His Finger [here the king placed the Gold Ring on the third finger of the prince's left hand], And also by delivering a Gold Rod into His Hand [at this point the king put into the prince's right hand the gold verge of government], That He may preside there and may direct and defend those parts to Hold to Him and His Heirs Kings of the United Kingdom of Great Britain and Ireland and of the British Dominions beyond the Seas for ever. Wherefore We will and strictly Command for Us, Our Heirs and Successors, That Our said Most Dear Son Edward Albert Christian George Andrew Patrick David may have the Name, Style, Title. Dignity, and Honour of the Principality of Wales and Earldom of Chester

aforesaid unto Him and His Heirs Kings of the United Kingdom of Great Britain and Ireland and of the British Dominions
beyond the Seas as is above mentioned. In witness whereof
We have caused these Our Letters to be made Patent. Witness
Ourself at Westminster the twenty third day of June in the
first year of Our Reign."

This was the wording used, albeit in former days in Latin,
in the investiture of Princes of Wales for centuries, which made
the ceremony all the more impressive. It was, as all must have
believed, the sign of the renewed vitality of the great state
to which the newly invested prince would be the heir. The
prince kneeled before the king, his sovereign, and before he
rose he gave once more the pledge which he had given in the
Abbey at Westminster a few weeks before.

"I, Edward Prince of Wales, do become your liege man of
life and limb and of earthly worship and faith and truth I will
bear unto you to live and die against all manner of folks."

When this moving act of homage had been performed the
king raised his son and heir from his knees, bestowing a kiss
on either of his cheeks, and placing in his left hand the letters-
patent. The prince then proceeded to his chair on the king's
right hand. In the address which followed from the people of
Wales, read by Sir John Rhys, there were many allusions to the
valour of the Welsh in helping to build the British Empire. The
prince, in his reply, used another of the Welsh sentences taught
him by Lloyd George: *Heb Dduw, heb ddim, Duw a digon—*
Without God, without anything, God is enough. He then
added, "I hope to do my duty to my king, to Wales, to you all."
So the prince who was both Edward and David came to the
land of his fathers and was presented, as the climax of the
ceremony, to the people. Three times did the king present the
prince to the people: first at the balcony over the Eleanor
Gate (so named from Eleanor, the Queen of Edward I and the
mother of the first Prince of Wales), secondly from the King's
Gate, and lastly in the Inner Bailey.

Thus opened a public career of immense hope, promise and
brilliance. It would be superfluous to attempt to describe
that career. There are, however, many who have grown up
during the period when that once-young prince has borne the

title of Duke of Windsor, and they cannot realize properly the immense burden of hopes from thousands of British people which rested upon him. To many he symbolised the power of a new Britain which would meet the challenge of the twentieth century, while not losing its ancient and proud traditions. He was the one who cared for the ex-serviceman and the unemployed. He was the acknowledged ambassador of Empire, the patron of trades and institutions, hitherto hardly touched by royalty; one who could be expected to do the unconventional thing.

On 20th January 1936, twenty-five years after that great day at Caernarvon, the Prince of Wales became King Edward VIII. On 10th December in the same year he renounced the throne for himself and his descendants, and this was confirmed by the Declaration of Abdication Act on 11th December. The latter was the day of the month on which James II, the last male Stuart to reign, was held by the government to have abdicated his throne.

What is this office which holds such romance in its very title, and the holders of which have evoked such varied sentiments in the people over whom they have been called to rule?

It is the purpose of this book to answer these questions and to give a full account of the Princes of Wales—their history, office, education, and the legends attached to them.

Briefly, the title comes from those rulers of North Wales, the Princes of Wales, of whom more will be said presently. The origin of the title is given in the well-known story of Edward I, after his conquest of Wales in 1284, offering the recalcitrant Welsh a prince of their own who could not speak a word of English and then bringing before them his infant son, the future Edward II, in swaddling clothes, a newly born child. Research has made great strides in sixty years. Dr. Doran, writing in 1860, retells the familiar story without a moment's hesitation, but authors of the decade 1910–1920 treat it as legend. Certain it is that the first Prince of Wales was born at Caernarvon Castle, was named Edward of Caernarvon and was made Prince of Wales, the first of the line. May it not have been that there was a presentation of the infant son to the Welsh chiefs, even though the formal creation came in 1301 when the Prince was seventeen?

Three hundred years ago the matter was in doubt and uncertainty. John Selden, in his *Titles of Honour* (1631), said that some regarded Edward I himself as the first Prince of Wales on the ground that he had been so created by his father, Henry III, in imitation of the Spanish title, Prince of the Asturias, because of his marriage to the daughter, Eleanor, of Alfonso X of Castile. Selden goes on to say: "Others place the beginning of this Title in Edward, son and heir to Edward the First, upon that known story of the kings sending for Queen Eleanor, being with child, out of England to be delivered at Caernarvon. After she was delivered, he engaged himself (they say) to the Welsh that they should have a prince most free from all kind of blemish on his honour, and one that could not speak one word of English, meaning this young prince. And it is true indeed that this Edward, son and heir apparent of Edward the First, was afterwards styled Prince of Wales, as we see in the Writs of Summons of him to the parliaments of the later time of his father. The direction to him is: Edwardo Principi Walliae, et Comiti Cestriae filio suo charissimo. But the first Charter of Creation that I have seen is that of King Edward the Third to his son and heir apparent Edward Duke of Cornwall, about five years after he was made Duke."

The stories of the second prince, Edward the Black Prince, also abound in romance, and foremost among those learned in childhood and painfully and unwillingly discarded in later life is that of the Black Prince's exploit at Crécy in 1346. There, we have been told, the prince was hard pressed in the battle, but won his spurs and in the triumph of English arms saw all his enemies prostrate. Among the slain was the blind King of Bohemia, who lay dead with the bridles of his two knights entwined with his. His crest was the famous ostrich feathers, and his motto *Ich Dien*. The Black Prince took these for himself, and so they have brought a heritage of glory to the succeeding princes.

Unfortunately historians and antiquaries have turned their sacrilegious hands to this tale also. It was William Camden in his *Remaines* who first gave currency to the story, and in his first version the battle where the crest was gained was Poitiers, later becoming Crécy. Camden did not give any authority for the statement, but in fact a contemporary manuscript does allude to the tale—contemporary, that is, with the Black Prince's time. This manuscript was a treatise on medicine by John Arderne, who was leech at the court and in the service of Edward III. Arderne attended the English army in France and was highly regarded in the suite of the Prince of Wales, the Black Prince, receiving a grant of land in Ireland in recognition of his services. Finally, it may be noted that Arderne's treatise did not have the story in all the copies of the manuscript but that it appeared in a copy which contained a chapter on haemorrhoids, where, writing in Latin, Arderne said: "And it should be observed that such a white feather was borne by Edward the eldest son of Edward King of England above his crest, and that he won that feather from the King of Bohemia whom he slew at Crécy in France, and thus took to himself the feather, which is called *Ostrich Fether*, which that most noble king had borne on his crest." Arderne then goes on to say that he wrote in the year 1376. To all of which the celebrated antiquary, Sir Harris Nicholas, commented: "There is therefore undoubtedly the statement of a contemporary who from his situation was likely to be well informed on the subject that the Black Prince took the Ostrich Feather from the crest of the King of Bohemia, whom he slew at Crécy, and assumed it for his own crest; but, though this assertion is entitled to great weight, I am not, I confess, convinced of its accuracy; and I still expect that proofs will some day be found that the Ostrich Feather and the mottoes 'Ich Dien' and 'Houmont' were derived from the prince's maternal house of Hainault."

It looks very much, therefore, as though the romances which have not unnaturally gathered around the Princes of Wales are fabrications, which have grown up in course of time. Yet even if all these stories were to be given up—and on the score of those mentioned more will be said later—there are so many true stories about the Princes of Wales that it is impossible for the most prosaic writer not to convey the feeling of chivalry and historic grandeur to his readers.

Several holders of the office or rank of Prince of Wales have met with untimely deaths. The first Prince of Wales, Edward of Caernarvon, was cruelly murdered at Berkeley Castle, at the end of a reign marked by continual misfortune. One of the most illustrious holders of the title, the Black Prince, never inherited the throne, but predeceased his father, Edward III. Richard II—one of the two Princes of Wales who have been the grandsons, not the sons, of the previous monarch—was also murdered after he had been deposed. The son of Edward IV was the luckless Edward V, one of the little princes in the Tower. The son of the king whom Edward IV had deposed, Henry VI, was himself murdered or otherwise slain after the battle of Tewkesbury. Richard III's son, another Edward, was dead by the age of eleven. The eldest son of George II never ascended the throne.

In two cases the deaths of Princes of Wales may not unfairly be said to have altered radically the course of history. Arthur, elder son of Henry VII, died before he was sixteen and was succeeded in title and in marriage by his brother, Prince Henry. Everyone knows the consequences of Henry's marriage with his brother's widow, Catherine of Aragon. Prince Henry, the elder son of the Scots King of England, James I, was a youth of great promise, but died when he was nineteen, and gave place to his younger brother, afterwards Charles I.

Two tragic cases, apart from those mentioned already, were those of the Old and the Young Pretender. The former was that son of James II of warming-pan fame. His birth was the innocent cause of the outbreak which his father's bigotry had prepared. The nation was ready to endure, if necessary, James II for the term of his natural life, but the thought of a son and successor who would be a Papist was too much. It became almost an article of faith that the young Prince of Wales could not be James II's true son but a foundling surreptitiously smuggled into the palace in the warming-pan. However, the Old Pretender was all his life in exile, after his earliest days, and gave to his own eldest son the title of Prince of Wales, an empty dignity for that hapless prince, Bonnie Prince Charlie. If the life of Charles Edward Stuart—the Young Pretender— could have ended after Culloden he would have left behind him one of the fairest names in true romance. Thus it can be seen that the Princes of Wales have partaken to the full in the ups and downs which have occurred in the history of the dynasties of Britain. One of the purposes of this book will be to recount the story in as much detail as space will permit.

Before beginning the study, however, it will be as well to clear the subject of the titles held by the eldest son of the reigning sovereign. The full title at present of the Prince of Wales is: H.R.H. Prince Charles Philip Arthur George, Prince of Wales and Earl of Chester, Duke of Cornwall in the Peerage of England, Duke of Rothesay, Earl of Carrick and Baron of Renfrew in the Peerage of Scotland, Lord of the Isles and Great Steward of Scotland. Whence did these titles come?

The title of Duke of Cornwall dates from 1337 when Edward III made his eldest son, then Earl of Chester, Duke of Cornwall, with remainder to his heirs, being the eldest sons of the Kings of England. By this charter the eldest son of the sovereign becomes from birth, or from the accession of his parent, Duke of Cornwall. Selden remarks: "By this creation not only was the first-born son of the Kings of England, but the eldest living also are always Dukes of Cornwall. Neither needed there any new creation of the title, although sometimes we find it joined with the creation of the title of Prince of Wales." The type of case to which Selden refers is that of Henry V, who, when his father became king as Henry IV, was created at once Prince of Wales, Earl of Chester and Duke of Cornwall. This, however, came about only because his father had suddenly become king, and Henry V had not been expected to be heir to the throne.

The titles in the Peerage of Scotland come to the eldest son of the sovereign because he is the heir of the old kingdom of Scotland as well as of England. Here again the learned Selden writes: "The prince and heir apparent there [i.e. Scotland] they style the Prince of Scotland, and the rest of the king's children they call also princes, as in other nations. The Prince of Scotland is as Prince, Duke of Rothesay, and High Steward of Scotland. And this Duchy of Rothesay was also the first Duchy there."

The title of Great Steward of Scotland is interesting because it was the Stuart ancestor of Prince Charles who was High

Steward of Scotland and whose issue became Kings of Scotland. Marjorie, daughter of Robert the Bruce, married Walter, the sixth High Steward of Scotland, and their son became Robert II and ancestor of the royal line of Stuart.

The title of Lord of the Isles recalls a very stormy part of Scottish history. The Clan Donald was headed in medieval days by the Lord of the Isles, meaning the western isles off the Scottish coast. In 1354 John, son of Angus Og, assumed the title of Dominus Insularum. He considered himself in a very special position and hardly as a vassal of the King of Scots. When they felt themselves able to take an independent course, the Lords of the Isles would throw off allegiance to the king seated in Edinburgh and conduct themselves as independent sovereigns. The story of Scottish freedom is a bitter tale of treacheries from within which mightily aided the assaults of foes from without, be those foes the Southron or the Norseman. The lordship of the Isles existed from 1354 to 1493, and the last Lord of the Isles did not hesitate to make a treaty with King Edward IV of England, acting in independence of the Scots king. By this treaty Scotland when conquered was to be partitioned between the Lord of the Isles, who was to take the northern Highland and the Isles, while the Earl of Douglas was to receive a further substantial portion of the realm, Edward of England naturally receiving the rest. This treaty being revealed to the King of Scots, he forced the Lord of the Isles to resign to the Crown some of his territories, and also to accept the lordship from the Scottish Crown. Previously it had been a title taken by the lords themselves, but after 1476 it was in the form of the usual feudal grant from the Crown. It was therefore revocable, and when further trouble with the Lord of the Isles took place the title was forfeited, and in 1493 it passed to the Scottish Crown. Hence the romantic title borne by the Prince of Wales.

In the past the sovereign's eldest son has had other titles, and a mention of them gives a retrospect of English history. There were those titles of Duke of Aquitaine, Earl of Ponthieu, and Monstroile, and Duke of Normandy. These honours go back to the old days when for several hundreds of years the Kings of England were more concerned about their possessions in

France than ever they were with England or other parts of the British Isles. Had the kings after Edward I given as much energy to the conquest or unification of the British Isles as they did to vain efforts in France the United Kingdom would have come into being much earlier. The connection with France began, of course, when a Duke of Normandy won the throne of England on the battlefield of Hastings. William, Duke of Normandy, was the vassal of the King of France. The forebears of William were the ravaging Norsemen from whom Normandy was named. The King of France had been compelled to allow Rollo the Ganger to take over one of his fairest provinces and to receive his homage as Duke of Normandy. Yet, strange to relate, when the Norse leaders had become nominally Christian dukes they were much better vassals to the French king than some of his other peers, such as the Dukes of Brittany. William the Conqueror was quite a good vassal to his suzerain. But once the dukes had become Kings of England they felt very keenly the change in their position. Under feudal law it was necessary for the vassal to render homage at stated periods to his overlord. It was one thing to do this as Duke of Normandy, but very irksome to perform the same duty when in another capacity the duke was a king. As King of England William the Conqueror received the homage of the barons of his realm and also acknowledgment of supremacy from the Welsh princes and the King of Scots. A potentate in his position did not much relish having to cross the Channel and give homage to the French king. As a matter of fact quarrels arose between William and his overlord, and William's death occurred while he was engaged in ravaging French territory. Under William's great-grandson the position became very much worse. Henry II of England married the divorced wife of the King of France. Being divorced, Eleanor of Aquitaine had to take back with her her dowry which included a great range of territories in the south-west of France. In right of his father, Henry was Count of Anjou; Maine and Normandy came from his mother's side. Now, through his wife's possessions, he ruled over land in France from the English Channel to the Pyrenees. Yet for these immense French possessions, which were larger than the lands ruled directly by the King of France, Henry had to do homage to the French king. This possession or loss of possession of French territories was to bedevil English and French politics for three hundred years. Normandy was conquered by the French in 1204, and by a treaty between English and French Crowns the titles and claims of the English king to Normandy were given up and so the queen is not correctly styled Duchess of Normandy. Under Edward III a new development took place, and the King of England actually assumed the title of King of France, and quartered the French arms in his shield. This use of the title went on for 460 years until in 1800, on the occasion of the Union between Great Britain and Ireland, the usage was changed. Edward III's main effort was to free himself from the degrading act of homage for his French territories. This he accomplished in the Treaty of Bretigny in 1360, after twenty years' fighting which devastated France. In the end the French refused to let the English control some of their choicest provinces and, under Joan of Arc, finally drove the English from France. Calais remained the only English continental possession and this fell in 1558. Yet the memory of French holdings lingered on and it was not until the coronation of George III that the representative figures of the Dukes of Aquitaine and of Normandy made their last appearance. This was in 1761. So high was the regard for these reminders of a lost dominion that these personages ranked before the Archbishop of Canterbury. Their natural position would be there, as had they been real they would have been princes of the blood.

In very ancient times, under the Saxon or Old English kings, the heir apparent was styled Clito, and the other sons Clitones or Clitunculi. This term is supposed to have come from the ancient Greek klutos—and indeed under the rule of the early English kings there was an affectation of Greek in regard to titles. Thus Athelstan, the grandson of Alfred the Great, who is termed in his charters Rex totius Britanniae, used also the term Basileus or Greek king, and this term is applied to other Kings of England before the Conquest. Another term frequently used for the heir to the throne in Saxon times is Atheling, and most of us have indistinct memories of references to Edgar Atheling. The term Atheling was almost the equivalent of *nobilis*, and in some of King Alfred's renderings from the Latin of Bede's history this comes out. It grew, however, to be restricted to the heir to the throne. After the Norman Conquest the heir to the throne was still termed Atheling, as in the case of William, the son of Henry I, who was drowned in the loss of the White Ship.

Thus the Prince of Wales has, behind his title, the accumulated history of ages, summing up the vicissitudes of the English race. More than once we have passed from empire to littleness, but always we have risen again because nothing can, in the words of Shakespeare, make us rue if England to herself do rest but true.

The Earldom of Chester is an ancient title in England, and represents the Palatine County of Chester. The term Palatine comes from the Latin *palatinus* and was applied under the later Roman Empire to officials attending on the emperor or carrying out duties at his court. It came to denote in the Eastern Byzantine Empire officials who were administrators of finances and imperial lands. Under the Frankish kings in France the term was applied to a *comes palatinus*, who carried out many duties assigned by the king. The Count Palatine became somewhat of an institution in various parts of western Europe and, with the Norman Conquest, was introduced into England. Here it was a term used to denote, in the form county palatine, a county which was outside the normal administration. In England the palatine counties were facing the boundaries of the country with Wales, Scotland and France. Thus the counties palatine were Chester, Durham, and possibly Kent. The earldom of Chester was given to Hugh, surnamed or nicknamed Lupus, from his rapacity, by William the Conqueror, and in his family it continued with one or two deprivations until 1232, when it lapsed to the Crown. From 1232 to 1237 it was held by John le Scot, Earl of Huntingdon, nephew of William the Lion, King of Scotland. On his death it was annexed to the Crown, and in 1254 was given to the Prince Edward, son of Henry III. From 1264 (after the king's defeat by Simon de Montfort at Lewes) Prince Edward had to resign his earldom to de Montfort in exchange for that of Leicester. He held it again after de Montfort's defeat and death at

Evesham in 1265. On Edward's accession to the throne the earldom merged in the Crown. From that time it was granted only to the eldest surviving son of the sovereign, and an Act of Richard II (1398) made it law for the earldom to belong to the sovereign's eldest son. This Act was repealed under Henry IV, but in fact the earldom has never been granted since then except in conjunction with the Principality of Wales. By this same Act of Richard II the earldom had been erected into a principality. The title of Prince of Wales is not that of a peer, but the peerage of Chester gives the prince the right to a seat in the House of Lords, though as a minor he will not occupy it until he is twenty-one. Royalty, or rather the heirs to the throne, are deemed to become of age at eighteen, but for purposes other than connected with their position as heirs apparent they do not come of age until twenty-one, like other persons.

By the foundation statutes of the Order of the Garter the Prince of Wales automatically becomes a Knight of the Order; though again, the taking of his place among the knights is deferred until he is of age suitable for investiture.

There is no office, as such, for the Prince of Wales, nor does the title bring with it any participation in state affairs even when the prince is older than the teenage period during which the honour has usually been bestowed. It is, however, obvious that so distinguished a personage as the Prince of Wales must from early years receive a tuition in affairs of state which will fit him for succession to the throne in due course. The education of the Prince of Wales will therefore be a matter of consideration in this book, and the different patterns which this has assumed down the centuries will be brought out.

One final matter remains to be considered in this Introduction: that is the subject of the Prince of Wales's arms. The arms as borne by the last Prince of Wales before the present holder were laid down by King George V. This was in 1911, when a warrant was issued to alter the arms of the Prince of Wales. Hitherto the Princes of Wales of the House of Hanover had borne the royal arms with the usual labels of difference, and with overall in the middle of the shield an inescutcheon showing the arms of Hanover. The new coat as set out in 1911 allowed full weight for the representation of Wales in the arms of its prince. The prince bore the royal arms, namely England 1 and 4 quarters, Scotland 2, and Ireland 3. Over all was an inescutcheon quarterly gules and or four lions passant guardant counterchanged, ensigned with the coronet befitting his degree. The label of difference on the royal arms was of three points argent.

The most interesting point here is that the shield in the middle of the prince's arms was that of the famous Prince of North Wales, Llywelyn the Great, who reigned 1194–1240.

Arms were anciently assigned to all persons of regal rank, and hence many of the ancient Welsh princes have had arms given to them in old armories, but there is no reason to doubt the authenticity of Llywelyn's arms, for he lived in the full heyday of the institution of heraldry.

CHAPTER II

The Ancient Princes of Wales

How came there to be a title of Prince of Wales at all?
John Selden gives the answer: "It was transferred from
those Princes of Wales (of North Wales especially) that,
in the elder times being Welsh, held the country under the
Kings of England, by the name of Princes. Neither was there
any other besides them to whom the peculiar Title of Prince
was attributed, as it is a subordinate dignity, Princeps Walliae
and Dominus Snowdoniac, was their usual title." Whence
came these Welsh princes?

To answer that we must recall some schoolday history.
We were told that the ancient Britons had been either extermin-
ated by the invading Saxons or else driven from the lowlands
of Britain into the western mountains. This account rests
partly on one literary reference; partly, and much more certainly, on archaeological evidence. There can be no doubt that
the cities of Roman Britain gradually fell before the Saxons.
This was in the period after A.D. 411, when officially the
Romans withdrew. In fact what happened was that after that
date the Roman officials ceased to be appointed from Rome
and there were no more regular troops in the island. Then
the Romano-British provincials found themselves assailed from
three sides: the Picts and Scots from the north, the Irish pirates
from the west, and the Saxons from the east. Between all these
forces it is marvellous how long the Britons resisted. They did
not supinely give way but fought hard for their land. Utoxeter
and Anderida (Pevensey) are two of the places which clearly
were taken by storm. Other cities such as Verulamium seem
to have been abandoned. What happened at London cannot
be known. Darkness descends over the city of London from the

Roman times about 411 until in the eighth or ninth century we find the Saxons in full occupation. The story goes that the city was abandoned—and it may have been; but if so, it would be interesting to know why it was afterwards occupied by the Saxons, who did not care to live in places where the Britons had dwelt.

It will never be known how thorough was the destruction caused by the English Conquest. It may be that the cities were abandoned but that many folk lived on in the countryside and survived the new rulers. It would be reasonable to assume that slaves and women were preserved, but, on the other hand, savage conquerors have been known to massacre for the sake of killing. How hard the invading English were can be gauged by the fact that to this day the other races who live in Britain have an innate prejudice against the Saxon or Sassenach. When they deride him it is really only the tribute of hatred, borne down long centuries, from the days when his galleys and other ships spelt ruin and desolation to the older inhabitants of the land. Between the fifth and the eighth centuries the English wrung from the Britons the whole of what we call England, except perhaps Cumberland or Cornwall, and also won the lowlands of Scotland, where Edwin's burgh is a reminder of an English King of Northumbria. The survivals of British power were in the Devon-Cornwall peninsula, in Wales, and in western Scotland. Wales and the Welsh derive their name from a typical English outlook. The native inhabitants of the land were the weallas or strangers to the English. It is curious how a nation preserves its essential characteristics. The fierce tribesmen from western Germany in the fifth century appear to have had little in common with the cultured English proconsul of the nineteenth or twentieth centuries, but the latter would often speak of himself as alone, when in the midst of multitudes of natives, whom he had somewhat disparagingly described as just that.

After the English conquest of England the land was organised into seven kingdoms, those of the heptarchy. Northumberland was one, Mercia (roughly the Midlands of England), Kent and Wessex are the most notable and those which have left their names on history. The kings of these lands claimed descent from Woden, the supreme god of their pantheon. They were of course pagans, although they did not long or very strenuously resist the teachings of Christianity. As the great Pope Gregory remarked in the famous story, *Non Angli sed angeli*, there is something in the English character, some *anima naturaliter Christiana*, which makes the acceptance of Christian teaching, at least moral teaching, easy. Among the kingdoms of the heptarchy there was a shifting struggle for supremacy. It went for a time, to King Edwin of Northumberland. He became a Christian, he drove the Welsh from Elmet (i.e. Leeds). He invaded Wales, in the sense of the Wales we know. He conquered Anglesey and Man, and earned himself a permanent niche in Welsh detestation by his campaigns. So greatly did the Welsh hate him that they combined with the pagans of Mercia to defeat and slay him. But their victory was short-lived, for in not many years after the death of Edwin another King of Northumberland, Oswy, slew Penda and utterly defeated the Welsh and Mercian alliance. Thereafter there was no hope of winning back Britain to the old race. This was in 655. Oswy, who died in 671, "was recognised", says Sir John Lloyd, "by Saxon, Angle, Briton, Pict and Scot as the supreme ruler of Britain, and after his death a good part of his authority was retained by his son Egfrith". I do not propose to trace the history of the struggles between Welsh and English but only to give the highlights, for without an understanding of these it is not possible to understand what the title of Prince of Wales means today.

From 655 dates the demarcation of a people quite different from the English. It means that after two hundred and fifty years the island was understood to be permanently lost to the descendants of the native Celts, and that the best they could hope for would be to hold their own in the lands left to them. A plausible motif for English history could be the attempts made throughout to subjugate the Celt. At any rate, in Wales the attempt was to be made several times during the period of six hundred years between the defeat of Penda and his Welsh allies and the conquest under Edward I.

Offa, King of Mercia, who died in 796, was to hand down his name to posterity in no uncertain fashion. He decided to leave a monument of practical value behind him. From sea to sea—from the Irish Sea to the Bristol Channel—he built a dyke which was to serve two purposes. It was to act as an announcement to the Welsh that they were not to trespass into Mercia. It was also an announcement to them that they need not fear permanent settlement by the English in Wales. In other words, it was a clear intimation that conquest had passed and co-existence was to obtain. Offa's greatness was even recognised by a mighty ruler in western Europe, Charles the Great. He treated with Offa as an equal. Offa ruled over Mercia, some twelve or more counties of present-day England. Yet his power was considerable, for he felt justified in using in one of his documents the famous phrase, *Rex totius Anglorum patriae*, King of all England. He reigned from 757 to 796, and his descent was traced from a namesake who had reigned over the English in their old home four hundred years before in what is now Schleswig. An interesting reminder of Offa's power is preserved in the old parish church of Bexhill, where a stone commemorates the fact that Offa was in some sense the over-lord of this part of Sussex.

After Offa's time the supremacy passed to Egbert of Wessex, who is given in the Anglo-Saxon Chronicle the title of Bretwalda or Ruler of Britain. He died in 839, and his grandson, Alfred the Great, had to fight very strenuously to keep even Wessex from the invading Danes. At last he gained the victory and in 878 succeeded in bringing the Danes to defeat and to acknowledge his sway. At the same date there died Rhodri Mawr, the Great. He had succeeded in uniting all Wales under his sway. He divided Wales, however, among his six sons, a practice understood in Welsh law but which merely undid all the good work which Rhodri's conquests had achieved. The Welsh princes submitted themselves to Alfred, whose object was to stand out as the Christian king, the bulwark and protector of all Christians in Britain against the heathen Danes. "The basis was laid of the homage which in later ages was regularly demanded from all Welsh princes by the English Crown" (Sir John Lloyd, *History of Wales*, page 328). It is perfectly clear from pre-Norman Conquest history that both Welsh princes and Scottish kings were in the habit of rendering homage to the English king, and William the Conqueror merely followed precedent in demanding this homage as the successor of the old English kings.

It was the weakness of Welsh law and custom which allowed the realms won by Rhodri Mawr to be divided among his sons. From his eldest son, Anarawd, descended the Princes of Powis, who were to be the last holders of the title Prince of Wales. From his second son, Cadell, came the line of Gruffyd ap Llywelyn, a prince who, like his ancestor, Rhodri, was able for a while to combine all Wales under his sway. Indeed, so powerful did Gruffyd become that much of the land across the dyke built by Offa was taken over by him. He lived in the reign of Edward the Confessor (1042–1066), and that good-natured but weak prince allowed him to hold under his rule large areas of English settlement in Cheshire and along the borders of Herefordshire.

But there stood at Edward's right hand an earl of very different temperament. This was Harold, a great soldier who was destined to perish at Hastings but not before he had given proof of his outstanding military qualities. He refused to tolerate Gruffyd's supremacy over English soil. By Harold's skilful direction the Welsh prince was cooped up in the mountains of the north. South Wales deserted him and the forces of Harold and his brother Tostig met in the north of the country. Gruffyd had many enemies, some of whom now brought about his downfall. Gruffyd's head was brought to Harold. The lightly armed English troops had penetrated all over the country and had wrought great destruction in the land. Wales was not conquered, but the Welsh were forced to dwell once more in their own borders.

The feat of Harold in reducing the Welsh king who had humiliated King Edward was to raise him in the estimation of all Englishmen, and to help him to the Crown of England, but naturally Harold was detested in Wales. When the news of his defeat and death at Hastings reached Wales there was at first great rejoicing, but soon the Welsh had little cause to be thankful for the overthrow of their enemy. He was replaced by a far more deadly foe. William the Conqueror had no illusions about exacting tribute from Welsh and Scots, but he felt that more was needed and he made his way into Wales with a view to taking over that country, as he had done England. He had a harder struggle. Indeed he left the matter to his barons, who were given carte blanche to get what they could from the Welsh. For some thirty-five years the struggle went backward and forward. In the north of Wales the invaders made considerable progress at first, but it was to be in the south and on the eastern border that they were to carve out their greatest successes. The Normans had in truth resumed the struggle which the English had to a remarkable degree discontinued; they were trying to conquer the whole of Wales. Eventually, by 1100, the Welsh retained control of the north and centre of the country, but had to face large Norman holdings in the south and a series of Marcher Lords along the borders of England and Wales. The fact that a Welsh county is named after one of the most famous Norman conquerors (Montgomeryshire) is proof enough that the Normans had made a deep indentation upon the country. They were, however, checked by the Welsh from the subjugation of the whole realm. Under Henry I (1100–1135) the land was nearly overcome and the Normans showed their usual skill in bringing the church of the conquered into submission so that the support of Rome was always on their side. This gave them an immense advantage.

None the less, after Henry I had been replaced by Stephen the Welsh rose once more in rebellion, and the resistance centred around the area known as Gwynedd, which for convenience may be called Snowdonia and adjacent territories. From the time of Stephen (1135–1154) there were princes of the line of Gwynedd who descended from Rhodri Mawr and who were worthy of their ancestor. Owain Gwynedd died in 1170, having successfully upheld the cause of Welsh independence against the power of Henry II (1154–1189). His grandson, Llywelyn Fawr, who died in 1240, married Joan, the daughter of King John. His grandson, again, was Llwelyn y Llyw Olaf; he married Eleanor de Montfort. He took sides in the wars between de Montfort and the English king, Henry III (1217–1272), but for his own advantage. When de Montfort had been defeated and slain, Llywelyn was still able

H.R.H. The Prince of Wales, 1969.

The traditional presentation of Edward of Caernarvon, as first Prince of Wales. *From the picture by Phil Morris, R.A.*

to extract from the English king a treaty which left him the position of Prince of Wales. This was in 1267. The Welsh prince had to do homage to the English king, but he won many concessions of land and was acknowledged as the chief prince in Wales, with any others as his vassals. The Prince of Wales might well have thought that he was now secure from English aggression, but he had not reckoned with the might of Edward I (1272–1307). No king in England's history has shown more power of development than Edward. The hot-headed youth of the battle of Lewes, who had lost the day by a headlong charge which he could not control, became the cool commander in the field, and the statesman administrator in the council chamber. True, he still gave way to fierce rages, but these only when some of his far-ranging plans miscarried through the fault of those who were less gifted than himself.

Edward I at the time of his succession to the throne was on a Crusade in Palestine, and it was not until 1274 that he was at home for his coronation. At that ceremony the Prince of Wales took no part. He did not render the homage required, nor pay the 3,000 marks a year which he had regularly sent in the late years of Henry III. Edward was not one to brook such conduct, and in 1276–1277 he waged war against Llywelyn with skill which forced the latter to shut himself up in his fortress of Snowdonia and face the prospect of starvation.

Llywelyn, perhaps with the fate two hundred years earlier of Gruffyd in mind, yielded and the Treaty of Conway gave him a much-lowered position. He was left with but five barons to be his vassals.

Yet even this signal defeat did not teach the Welsh prince a lasting lesson. A few years later, in 1282, he raised revolt once more and tried to rouse the whole of Wales against Edward. He took Edward by surprise, but the king was equal to the occasion. Once more he organised the subjugation of Wales. He sustained some reverses, but Edward was a soldier, not a knight errant, and could not be turned back from his purpose by a defeat.

Well aware of his enemy's skill, Llywelyn turned to the south of Wales to draw Edward away from the north and to rouse the flagging spirit of revolt. It was while he was in the region of the Wye valley that in a small skirmish Llywelyn met his end. His head was sent to London to prove the reality of Edward's triumph. Llywelyn left no heir, his brother David, who had been a favourite with the English until he joined in revolt against them, being captured and put to a cruel death. Llywelyn's only child was a girl, Gwenllian, born in the June before the death of her father. She was put into a convent by Edward and lived her life as a nun.

That was the end of the Princes of Wales of the Welsh line, and the end of the Welsh resistance. Edward found plenty of work to do in organising the conquest of Wales, but the end was foreknown. Then Edward had the task of keeping the country he had won. It was in the desire to do this that he brought his queen to Caernarvon that she might give birth to their child in Wales. Whatever may be thought of the old story that Edward presented his son to the Welsh, as their prince who could not speak a word of English, there is no doubt that Edward was much exercised over the problem of combining Welsh national feeling with centralised authority in Britain. Already Edward was planning the unification of all Britain, and he determined to bring this about by any means. He probably intended very early on to make his son, Edward, Prince of Wales, especially when the latter became his eldest surviving son by the death of the little Alphonso.

This, then, is the background of the title Prince of Wales. It is deep-rooted in the thousand-year-old tradition of the Welsh people, and for this reason the Prince of Wales can always look to the devotion of the people of his principality.

CHAPTER III

Edward of Caernarvon

THE first Prince of Wales, who was an Englishman, had
been well trained in the lessons of war and politics by
his father, and could hardly have had a better teacher.
Unfortunately the pupil was not remotely interested in the
lessons. When his father was alive Edward of Caernarvon had
been required to take his father's place on many occasions.
One instance had occurred when Edward I had had a considerable disagreement with his barons and it was deemed wise for
the king to absent himself in foreign war, while his son and
heir, the Lord Edward, met the barons and other magnates of
the realm. He had thus every opportunity of learning the
duties of a king. Unfortunately the dominant characteristics
of the Prince of Wales were dislike of labour, love of pleasure,
and a willingness to be led by anyone who happened to catch
his fancy. The scenes between father and son make very
unpleasant reading. It is hard to say who must have been the
more unhappy, Edward I or his son.

Early in life Edward II (it will be more convenient to refer
to him by his subsequent title) came into contact with Piers
Gaveston, one of the major influences in his career and certainly
one of the worst. Gaveston's entry into the royal household
came about through his father's good service in the wars of
Edward I. To reward his faithful knight, Edward I gave him
among other things the privilege of placing his son, Piers, in
company with the king's own son. From the start Edward II
doted on Gaveston. They grew up together, and it would seem
that they were for years nearly inseparable. The older writers
draw a veil over the inference which many modern writers
would naturally deduce from such a relationship. It may be,

35

of course, that the modern outlook is simply derived from facts which are either more apparent now or more abundant owing to the moral ill health of our age. I do not wish to take the characters of Edward II and Gaveston into greater infamy than would attend them in any case, but I am bound to mention the suggestion that they were perverts. If so, there are certain interesting features in the case. Edward II was a big man, of powerful physique; in fact, he was described as the strongest man of his realm, and must have been physically the equal of his father, whose nickname was Longshanks. If Gaveston was Edward's lover, the relationship would be explicable from the analogy of some cases where big athletic men care little for women but are enamoured of lithe, handsome, deft male personages. Then, again, a curious feature of the story is the marriage of both Edward and Gaveston. Edward married a noted beauty, Isabella the Fair, a princess of France. By her he had four children. Gaveston was married to the king's niece, the sister of the Earl of Gloucester. If these men were homosexuals, they must have been of the order of some others known to history, of whom Julius Caesar is the most famous or infamous. Caesar was indifferent whether boys or women were his object. He was a lover of all sexual pleasures, and Edward and Gaveston may have been the same.

However, there is enough in the character of Edward to excite disgust without definitely fixing the guilt of homosexual practices upon him; I merely mention these abnormalities as possible.

The title of Prince of Wales was conferred as the outward sign that the sovereign's son was his heir apparent and trained to succeed him. The principle of election of a sovereign is still remaining as a relic of the past in the coronation service when the sovereign is presented to his or her people and when they are asked if they will accept their new monarch. In bygone days the monarchy really was elective. Very rarely in English history throughout its whole length has a person not of royal blood been elevated to the throne. The only true case is that of Harold II, who fell at Hastings. Lady Jane Grey had the blood of Henry VII in her veins, and some sort of claim to the throne. Cromwell is usually placed among the sovereign rulers of England, but his case was certainly unique in so far that he made himself king or ruler. The election of the sovereign was therefore not from the whole people (as in the Biblical story of the choice of Saul, the son of Kish) but from the royal house. The ablest man or the one most acceptable to the people was chosen. In this way Alfred the Great was chosen in preference to the young sons of his elder brother. William the Conqueror chose his younger son, Rufus, instead of his elder, Robert, to rule England. Henry I's daughter Matilda was passed over by the barons in favour of Stephen, her cousin. From the time of Henry II (1154–1189) until that of Richard II (1377–1399) the lineal heir, whether eldest son, brother or grandson, succeeded, except in the case of Arthur of Brittany. He was the son of Geoffrey, the elder brother of King John, but his place was taken by John, probably with the full assent of the barons.

With the reign of Richard II the principle which was gradually being established of lineal succession was lost for a century. Richard was deposed and his place taken by his cousin, Henry IV. The latter had a troubled reign, and his grandson, Henry VI, was himself deposed and his throne taken by his cousin, Edward IV. The son of Edward IV, the little Edward V, had barely been seated upon the throne before he was displaced by his uncle, Richard III. It was only with the advent of the Tudors, in the person of Henry VII, that the principle of primogeniture was established, and the doctrine that the king never dies could be taken as a fact of constitutional law. "The king is dead, long live the king" (or queen), is the embodiment of this principle.

Taking Egbert of Wessex as the first King of England, about 825, we have six hundred years during which the principle of primogeniture was being established in the royal house. The adoption of the title of Prince of Wales for the sovereign's eldest son helped in this struggle. In every reign the first hope of a king would naturally be centred on his first-born or surviving son, and the need to bestow the title on the eldest surviving son would help to mark out that son as the destined king. It will be found that from the time when the title of Prince of Wales was instituted every sovereign has either

declared his eldest son Prince of Wales or intended to do so
(as in the case of Henry VIII and Edward VI, the latter never
being Prince of Wales), or been prevented from doing so by
the untimely death of the heir (as in the case of Queen Anne,
whose son, the Duke of Gloucester, died before he was twelve
years old).

Thus it is easy to see the formation of a principle: that the
title of Prince of Wales being in existence, it would be necessary
to bestow it upon the king's heir, and thus attention would be
focused upon the king's heir apparent, his eldest son. The
story is told of Edward II, that on one occasion he procured
the aid of the Bishop of Chester to plead with Edward I on
behalf of Gaveston that the title of Count of Ponthieu should
be bestowed upon the latter. Edward, who considered that
all his son's troubles stemmed from the influence of Gaveston,
flew into a rage, and, sending for Edward, gave him the full
vent of his temper. He seized the prince, tore out his hair in
handfuls, and even in his rage cast doubts on the chastity of
Queen Eleanor, Edward II's mother. Edward I cried out in
his frenzy of rage: "God alive! Were it not that the kingdom
might fall into anarchy, I would take care that thou shouldst
never come to thy inheritance." Edward I said this because
he had lost all his other sons by his first marriage.

In fact, of course, Edward I knew that Edward II had to
succeed him, and after he had banished Gaveston he tried by
the most dire means to make his son worthy of his future
position. No pains were spared on the young prince's education, but it was of no use; he simply was not the material which
makes a ruler. He was interested in various sports, such as
swimming, and he was a good knight in the lists. In Marlowe's
play about him there is a pathetic reminder of this at the end
when Edward in his misery and degradation exclaims:

> Tell Isabel the Queen, I looked not thus
> When for her sake I ran at tilt in France
> And there unhorsed the Duke of Clermont.

Edward was also good at hedging and ditching, and at
thatching houses—that is, of course, as a pastime. It seems

that, like other kings (compare Louis XVI, with his love of the blacksmith's forge), Edward took pleasure in pursuits of a handicraft nature, which probably pleased him more than his enforced duties of statecraft.

Edward's career can be told briefly. He accompanied his father on the latter's last journey northwards, in 1307, when he was seeking again to crush Scottish rebellion. Bruce was making some headway, but the aged Edward, then sixty-nine and one who had lived harder than most men, determined to overthrow what he regarded as the last flicker of Scottish independence. Eventually his ageing body proved too much even for Edward's iron will and he had to be carried on a litter until he reached Burgh on Sands, where he died. He gave the most specific instructions to his son not to bury his body until Scotland was subdued. How well Edward II kept this undertaking was soon clear. One of Edward's first acts on becoming king was to recall Gaveston. He longed for his friend. His next serious act, or rather his first act of state, was to retreat from Scotland and leave the English garrisons to their fate. Had he persevered he could have overthrown Bruce without undue effort, for that leader was far from strongly supported and was under a cloud, owing to the murder of his rival Comyn in a church. To salve his conscience, Edward took his father's body to London and entombed it in a splendid burial place in Westminster Abbey. There the body rests in its tomb, above ground, so that the letter of Edward I's instructions was observed. The body was, technically, not laid under ground, until Scotland should be subdued. For all practical purposes, Edward II gave up the Scottish war, and it was not until seven years had passed that he once more marched towards Scotland. By this time Bruce had become truly formidable.

The result of Edward's expedition is known to everyone. It is one of the recurrent themes of Scottish history and literature. At Bannockburn Bruce defeated Edward as no English army was ever defeated in medieval times. It was all that the English king could do to escape with his life and safety. Ignominiously he fled towards the English border, while behind him the wreckage of his army fought for life.

This was the result of Edward's neglect after seven years of rule, but even worse was to follow. Under the leadership of Bruce the Scots raided down into England as far as York. Eventually they were to dictate their terms at the Treaty of Northampton in 1328, whereby the English king agreed to recognise their independence. The result of the English defeat was to breed in English minds a determination to get even with the Scots and to conquer them if possible, while the Scots for their part were equally determined never to yield. An alliance was formed between Scotland and France whereby each was to do as much damage as possible to England, should either be attacked by the English.

Edward had been forced to part with his favourite Gaveston twice in the period between 1307 and 1312. On each occasion he had insisted on recalling Perot (his pet name for "his brother" Gaveston), and at last the barons decided to finish matters with the favourite. They seized and beheaded him. The leader of the insurgent barons was Thomas, the Earl of Lancaster, and a cousin of the king (Lancaster was grandson of Henry III). Although Edward grieved for Gaveston, he was not strong enough to avenge him, and had to submit to the rule of some of his lords.

After the disgrace of Bannockburn Edward turned for friendship and support to one of the barons who was friendly towards him. This was Hugh Despencer. The latter guided Edward's administration, while his son, also called Hugh, became a dear friend and very close to Edward, so as to compensate him for Gaveston's loss. The other barons had, of course, no more liking for the Despencers than they had for Gaveston, and in 1321 they managed to procure their banishment. But Edward was now determined to fight for his friends. He succeeded in defeating the barons and the Earl of Lancaster was beheaded. The Despencers then ruled England for five years. Hugh Despencer the younger was married to Edward's niece.

It was at this stage that the real cause of Edward's ruin appeared. His wife had borne with many indignities which hardly appealed to a proud French princess. Despite all that may be surmised about Edward and his male favourites, his queen was willing to tolerate the continuance of her marriage for at least ten years. Eleanor, the younger of the king's daughters, was born in 1318.

It was the growing dependence of the king upon the Despencers, rather than his habits of life which finally disgusted the queen with her husband. In 1325 she found ways and means to persuade Edward to let her go to the court of her brother, the King of France; and even more important, to take the young heir to the throne, Edward, with her.

Once she was in France the queen had no intention of returning until she was sure of ruling England. She refused to return until Edward should promise to give up his favourites. While a long argument went on between Isabella and Edward on this subject, the queen gathered a faction of exiled English lords and with these landed in 1326 in Essex. Her avowed purpose was to avenge the death of Lancaster and get rid of the Despencers. In fact, behind this avowed intention were sinister factors which threatened Edward's life and throne. The queen was a woman of great beauty and of passionate feeling. In France she had taken a lover, one of the English noblemen, Roger Mortimer, and he, of course, accompanied her to England.

The Despencers were, after all, only the favourites of a weak king, and they were easily disposed of. They were seized and put to death at Bristol. The king tried to escape, but was also captured and deposed, in a parliament at Westminster at the beginning of 1327, in favour of his son, Edward. The latter became king and was crowned on 29th January 1327. Meanwhile, his unhappy father was removed from one place of captivity to another, until at last he arrived at Berkeley Castle, where he was in the charge of two dependants of Mortimer. At Berkeley Castle, in September 1327, he was cruelly murdered. He was ill-treated and disgraced in every possible way in the hope that he would die of disease or accident, but his strength of body kept him from this, and so it was decided by the queen and Roger Mortimer that he must be murdered.

This was done by the fearful method of thrusting red-hot irons up his back passage, and thus killing him without signs of outward bloodshed. The character of Isabella can be gauged by the fact that she was willing to acquiesce in, even if she did not suggest, such an end for her husband.

The fallen king was said to have died a natural death and his body was buried in the abbey at Gloucester, now the cathedral. Then came one of those curious manifestations which show how little the English character has changed in the passage of many ages. It soon began to be rumoured that prayer at the dead king's tomb led to the granting of petitions, and even that miracles were wrought at his grave. The place became a centre of local pilgrimage. Leaving aside the difference in religious outlook between 1327 and 1958, it is not difficult to understand the changed feeling about Edward after his death. During his life he had not perhaps been more unpopular than his father. Edward I had often demanded much from his people in treasure and blood. Edward II asked little but the right to spend money on his dear friends. He had made little impact upon his people, and the stories about his conduct with Gaveston or the younger Despencer probably never reached the country districts. While no one had been willing to strike a blow for him against his queen and barons, when he lost his throne sympathy began to veer towards him. He was, in the common expression, down on his luck. There is a natural English dislike to "kicking a man when he is down". The facts of the murder could not long be concealed. The story goes that the horrible screams of the dying king could be heard from Berkeley Castle.

So there was the deposed sovereign, remorselessly cleared out of the way by his unfaithful wife and her lover. One can imagine the sentiment of the people. "After all, whatever his faults, he did not deserve that, to be murdered in cold blood. And that French queen, she's no better than she ought to have been. She and that lover of hers are ruling the young boy-king, and goodness knows what harm they will do the country." After which, as always happens in England, the dead king's abilities as a sportsman would be remembered. This probably tipped the scales in his favour, and the weak, self-indulgent monarch was in process of canonization.

This movement of popular opinion assisted the young king in his task of overthrowing Mortimer. He was only fourteen and a half years old when he became king. He can of course be acquitted of any desire to overthrow his father. For four years he was under the management of Mortimer and his mother. Then, in 1330, by careful arrangement with some of his nobles, Edward contrived to seize Mortimer in Nottingham Castle. Mortimer was found in a room near the queen's apartments. He was not given much time to meditate upon the change in his fortunes. A parliament was quickly summoned, and Mortimer's crimes were laid before it, including the charge that he had been the cause of Edward II's death. No trial or process occurred. Mortimer was roundly condemned and executed. The queen was retired from public life, and although Edward III paid her one or two visits each year she was without any further political or social influence.

From the time when he overthrew Mortimer Edward III began to reign. He was to be king for fifty years, to raise his country to a great position in Europe, and then to outlive both his glory and his eldest son.

Edward III was never created Prince of Wales, but only Earl of Chester and Duke of Aquitaine. He was as we have seen, not fifteen when he came to the throne, and his father may well have thought that he was too young to take the title of Prince of Wales, which at that time carried with it certain responsibilities of government, and also served to mark out the heir to the throne.

The subject of the age at which the Prince of Wales is to be created is one of the most awkward questions in the whole history of the princes. Edward of Caernarvon, the first prince, was seventeen years old when so created. The latest Prince of Wales received the title when he was nine and a half. Consequently there is no real guiding principle, especially when it is recollected that Edward III never received the title, whereas his own son, the famous Black Prince, became Prince of Wales at thirteen.

The only clue which can be given to the age when the Prince of Wales should be created is that there appears, especially in older days, to be a predilection for the early teens. The Duke of Windsor was thus almost exactly of the age of the first prince to be created. His father and grandfather, however, were right outside any of the recognised norms. George V did, of course, succeed his brother as heir apparent and, in any event, his father, Edward VII, did not succeed to the throne until George was thirty-five to thirty-six years old.

What was the education of a Prince of Wales really like in the fourteenth century? I have mentioned training in state-craft and in war. Some knowledge of the latter has been given to all princes in all ages. Towards the end of the fifteenth century there flourished a lady known as Dame Julyana Bernes or Berners, of whom very little is known save that she left behind her the volume which goes under the title *The Book of St. Albans*. She is supposed to have been Prioress of Sopwell, a nunnery near St. Albans, and in this abbey the book was first printed, hence the name usually given to the volume. The book contains a Treatise of Hawking, of Hunting, of Coat Armour, Fishing with an Angle, and Blazing of Arms. The work thus represents dissertation on some of the main accomplishments of the fifteenth-century gentleman.

Here were some of the accomplishments which were expected of a gentleman and, par excellence, of one destined to be king. The emphasis laid on sport is in accordance with English life in all ages, although the sports have altered in certain respects. Hawking has gone, why is not clear, but hunting is still the pastime of the leaders of society, while fishing is shared by high and low alike.

Hunting was more important in medieval times than now. It was then a means of replenishing the larder. There is something of truth in the saying of Freeman, in his *Norman Conquest*, that in Norman times hunting had not quite lost its character of a defensive war against nature. The provision of one of the Saxon kings that the Welsh should produce four hundred wolves' heads per year was part of this. By the times of the Plantagenet kings no such character of defence existed about hunting. Wolves still lingered in Scotland and Ireland (in both countries until the eighteenth century), and in Scotland the last bear was killed in the fifteenth century. But in England dangerous animals were extinct by the fourteenth century, or at least the wild cats and boars could not provide sufficient danger to the community. It was food which was the main feature in the absorption with hunting. Food brought in thus helped out the medieval household.

Hunting also served as the training ground for the rider and the warrior. It was an easier means of warfare, in a sense. Every knight—and the king was expected to be a good knight— had to be a good rider, and able to use sword, lance, axe, mace and the crossbow. The wearing of armour made many demands on the physique, and could only be endured by constant practice. Most of the Plantagenet princes loved warfare, and sought every opportunity of exercising them-selves in arms. The tournament was such an exercise. Edward I was described as the best lance in the world, Edward II was a skilled jouster, and Edward III was a knight of the highest quality. He loved tournaments and feats of arms of all kinds.

Thus the Prince of Wales of the fourteenth century was to be a soldier and sportsman and, in addition, a statesman and administrator. He was also required to be a good dancer, a performer on some musical instruments, and perhaps a singer. Nor was clerical education neglected. Edward III had a tutor, Richard de Bury or d'Aungerville, who en-deavoured to imbue him with a love of literature. Gone were the days when a king could be illiterate, and the Plantagenet princes were skilled men in reading, writing, and knowledge of languages. They had many things to learn in their education and often they learnt the hard way.

The first Viscount Falkland, who died in 1633, was a man of letters who left behind him a collection of papers which were printed in 1680 under the title: *The History of the most unfortunate Prince, King Edward II, with choice Political Obserfations on him and his unhappy Favourites, Gaveston and Spencer: containing several rare passages of those times, not found in other historians.*
This work contains an account of Edward's reign which is rather different from the accounts normally in the history books; for example, Bannockburn becomes Eastrivelyn. How-ever, it is in the accounts of the wretched king's private life that the noble author excels himself. He describes the defection of Edward's queen, Isabella of France, thus:

"The Queen, who had long hated the insolency of the Spencers, and pitying the languishing estate of the Kingdom, resolves in her mind all the possible ways to reform them. Love and Jealousy, two powerful motives, spurred her on to undertake it. She saw the King a stranger to her bed, and revelling in the embraces of his wanton minions, without so much as a glance or look on her deserving beauty. This contempt had begot in her impressions of a like, though not so wanton and licentious a nature. She wanting a fit subject for her affections to work on (her wedlock being estranged), had fixed her wandering eye upon the goodly shape and beauty of gallant Mortimer. He was not behind hand in the reception and comely entertainment of so rich and desired a purchase."

In the preface to the book, which is not written by Falkland, we have a description of Edward's death at Berkeley: "They took him in his bed, and casting heavy bolsters upon him, and pressing him down, stifled him; and not content with that, they heated an iron red hot, and through a pipe thrust it up into his fundament, that no marks of violence might be seen; but though none were seen, yet some were heard, for when the fact was in doing, he was heard to roar and cry all the castle over."

CHAPTER IV

Edward of Woodstock

Very early in life Edward III had been married to the Lady Philippa, the daughter of William, Count of Holland and Hainault. She was to prove a good and fruitful wife to him. She bore him nine sons and five daughters, and the eldest of these was the famous Edward, the Black Prince. It was not until after his lifetime that he was known as the Black Prince, allegedly from the colour of his armour, but possibly because of his fierce prosecution of war in France, where he left behind him a trail of burnings. He was called Edward of Woodstock, from the place of his birth. He was born on 15th June 1330, and very soon created Earl of Chester (when he was three), and Duke of Cornwall (when he was seven).

The dukedom of Cornwall was conferred upon the prince in 1337 and was the first dukedom to be created in England. The title by its patent was to descend to the heirs of the grantee, being the eldest sons of the sovereigns of England. By this charter the eldest son of the sovereign becomes from birth, or from his parent's accession to the throne, Duke of Cornwall.

The prince was made Prince of Wales in 1343, being then hardly thirteen. Yet young as he was, he had already begun to take his part in public life. At the age of seven, when he became a duke, he had conferred the honour of knighthood on twenty candidates. When he was eight and nine he had presided over Parliaments held at Northampton and at Westminster, his father being absent on the Continent. He travelled also, being only ten when his father held court at Antwerp in 1340, the year in which Edward III assumed the title of King of France. Then there were tournaments, of a milder nature than those of the fully adult, yet events in which the prince learned hard knocks. He was educated in clerkly arts by Dr. Walter Burley, of Merton College, Oxford. At another time he was left in nominal charge of the Tower of London.

In all these ways the boy learned about statecraft and war. When he became Prince of Wales his father was careful to put into his hands all the claims on the principality which he ought to possess. Incidentally, it is said that the title of Prince of Wales was conferred on Edward with the assent of the nobles, *par assent de touz les grauntz d'Engleterre*. This is the only instance of such an expression being used, as the bestowal of the title of Prince of Wales is a matter reserved for the sovereign alone.

Three years later the young prince was to cover himself with an undying glory at Crécy. He had thirsted for martial glory, and the reign of his father was the very epoch to provide him with the opportunity. How came this to be so?

From 1272 (the accession of Edward I) to 1377 (the accession of Richard II, great-great-grandson of Edward I) the English were never long at peace. During that time they fought the Welsh, the Irish, the Scots, the French, and the Spaniards. They fought the French and the Spaniards by sea and by land. They fought great battles, they conducted numerous sieges, they made vast marches over hostile territory, and in short they underwent every military experience. During the period under review they held huge stretches of land in other countries, albeit that at the end of their conquests they possessed only Wales, Ireland and Calais.

What was the cause of this aggressive energy? Under Edward I it had been the result of that king's ambition to make one realm of Britain politically as well as geographically. Under Edward III it was caused by very different factors.

Edward III, being the son of a princess of France who had no brother to leave surviving issue, considered himself to have a just claim to the Crown of France. We all know the arguments by which the wily Archbishop of Canterbury in Shakespeare's *Henry V* assures the king that the Salic law does not bar his claim from the throne of France. None the less the French had other views, and the kingdom of France went to a cousin's line, and Philip of Valois became king.

The black Prince, Edward the third's eldest sonn:
lives in this Peece and power; he that wonn
his Knighthood in the feild: and did aduaunce,
his Standard; through the trembling hart of Fraunce
that with eight thousand at Poicters gaue fight:
to threescore thousand; slewe and put to flight,
the whole army; and took prisoner their King.
when the braue Bow-men with ye gray goose winge
in all extreametyes; weare euer tried;
to draw home; and draw conquest to theire side:
with these hee ouerran a part of Spaine:
and gainst ye Bastard; calld King Pedro reigne
for which, vppon theire come wee yet perceaue:
of the broad English arrow: a full sheaf
2gr. Agincourts victorious battaile; shew,
what laurell sprange out of the trusty bow
Black weare the showre of arrows that day spent,
and yet, they hing shrill ric bric as they went.
the terror of his fights; the black Prince wonn
the name of Black; not his complexion.
This to his deathless memoryhee erected:
and to famous Archery; toe much neglected

Dedicated to all the worthy
and trew louers of
Archery.
The Cecill
Sculp:

HONI SOIT QVI MAL Y PENSE

ICK DIEN

POITTIERS

Daniel engraved Angell in Lombardstre:

Edward the Black Prince, Prince of Wales, 1343. Died before his father,
Edward III.

Richard, son of the Black Prince, Prince of Wales, 1377:
afterwards Richard II.

Edward III had had to present himself at Paris and render homage to his kinsman for his French possessions. Originally, after the Norman Conquest, England had been tied to France by reason of her king being Duke of Normandy. Henry II by marrying Eleanor of Aquitaine acquired even more French possessions.

The history of the English and French connections goes back to the time of William the Conqueror. The latter had been Duke of Normandy, and when he became King of England he was still bound as duke to render homage to his overlord, the King of France. The situation became much more difficult with succeeding reigns in England. Matilda, the Conqueror's granddaughter, married the Count of Anjou, and this brought Anjou as well as Normandy and Maine into relation to the English Crown. When Matilda's son, Henry II, succeeded to the throne, he was King of England, Duke of Normandy, Count of Anjou and of Maine.

Then Henry II married the divorced wife of the King of France, whose dower reverted to her on her divorce. She was Eleanor of Aquitaine, and brought this property to her new husband. Thus the rule of the English king stretched from the English Channel to the Pyrenees, taking in also Brittany, where one of Henry's sons had married the Duchess of Brittany.

The situation was farcical for both English and French kings. The English sovereign had to render homage to his overlord for half the latter's territory. The English possessions in France cut off the French king from the whole of the western seaboard of France. From the French point of view it was essential to get rid of this vast intrusion into French lands. The first step to this liberation of France came when the French king turned King John out of Normandy in 1204.

Yet the English king still retained the right to the lands in the south-west, Gascony and Aquitaine. For these he was required to give feudal homage to the French king. Edward III had to do this, and found it highly unpleasant.

At the beginning of his reign Edward III warred in Scotland and it looked as though he would renew his grandfather's efforts to conquer that country. The determining factor in turning the English king towards France was the aid given by the French king to the Scots in their wars with the English. To rid himself of the homage, galling to him and to his people, and to crush those who helped his Scottish foes, was Edward's object in beginning war with France.

It is hard to say how serious was Edward's intention when in 1340 he assumed the title of King of France, and took the lilies of France into his shield of arms. Perhaps he hoped by the very extremity of his claim that the French would seek to propitiate him by making some concession. He could hardly have been quite serious about a claim to all France, even had it been legal, for the subjugation of so vast an area was beyond his power.

However, the failure of the French king to appreciate Edward's point of view led him to embark on a long war of over twenty years with France. Indeed this war was really to last for more than a hundred years. From 1340 until 1453 it went on, with enormous devastation in France, and also with misery to England.

Possibly Edward's real object in waging war with the French was to secure freedom from the necessity of rendering homage for his ancestral French lands.

The first round in the battle began with a victory at Sluys, on the coast of Holland. This was a sound move, for, by destroying the French fleet, the English king secured control of the narrow seas and could bring his armies across without danger of interception. In fact, this was a typical move of a nature to be repeated again and again in subsequent centuries, right down to the invasion of 1944.

The young prince was in England when this naval battle was fought and had to be content with his father's description of the battles contained in his despatches. The mastery of the Channel being secured, the English invaded France. Part of the king's strategy, in securing allies, has a familiar sound. Command of the sea, and allies on the Continent against the predominant power, has thus been part of English strategy from the days of Edward III until now.

For the first six years of the conflict Edward manœuvred, marched and counter-marched across northern France. No great battles were fought, though the English were able to intervene in Brittany, and to help their allies in Flanders, while hosts of Germans, attracted by the thought of war and plunder, hovered on the borders of France.

Then, in 1346, came the turn of both Edward III and the Black Prince. The latter was now sixteen years old, and considered of age to lead his men in battle. Edward endeavoured to escape the pursuing French hosts by crossing the river Somme when the bridges had been broken down, and only with the greatest difficulty could a ford be found.

"Let him that loves me follow me," was Edward's exhortation, and, accompanied by his son, he plunged into the Somme, while his army followed.

Once across, he found himself still faced by the huge army of the French which barred further progress. There was no alternative but to fight against greatly superior numbers. It is said that the English were thirty thousand men and the French four times their number. Numbers were very difficult for the medieval chronicler to assess, and there were certainly mistakes in numbering. The French army was, however, without doubt greatly superior in numbers. Edward seems not to have been worried over the outcome. He remained watching the contest in a mill, while he had entrusted the management of the first English division to the Black Prince.

The young Prince was assisted by the presence with him of two very experienced commanders, the Earl of Warwick, and the great knight, Sir John Chandos. Yet, despite this, it sheds some considerable light on the education of a Prince of Wales in the fourteenth century that a boy of sixteen could have been left to fight in the thickest of the battle. Of course, he had been trained as few boys of today, even with the roughest upbringing, have been trained. For one thing, his frame was inured from an early age to wear armour, and he was used to the management of the knightly weapons, sword and axe, lance and mace.

The story of the battle at Crécy is well known. The French sent their Genoese mercenaries in to the attack, but these were soon in great difficulties. They not only found English opposition very tough but were unfairly assailed by the French. Like men devoid of any idea of tactics, the latter swept into

the attack. They were smitten by arrow storms, and overthrown by maces, swords and spears. Yet still they came on, and
the vastness of their numbers made it a matter for wonder how
long the English division could hold.

Appeal was made to the king. "Is my son killed, wounded,
overthrown, or badly bested?" "No, sire, but he is in the
thick of the battle." "Then let the boy win his spurs, for I
intend that the glory of the day shall be his." So runs the
immortal dialogue, and with the great words, "let the boy
win his spurs", the English were heartened and set about the
French with renewed vigour.

By nightfall, after a grim August day, the French were in a
broken condition, and even their king found it as well to ride
from the field with a few followers. The victory was Edward's,
and it had been won by the valiant prince.

The meeting between king and prince was marked by great
affection. Seldom could any father have felt as proud as
Edward, while his pleasure was heightened by the noble
bearing of his son. The prince was without a trace of vain-
glory, and bore himself with deep humility.

Soon the prince was home in England, where his popularity
knew no bounds. His father wisely determined to let the
prince make request for anything which was needed for carrying
on the war. The Parliament and the City of London refused
nothing to the hero of the hour.

There have been Princes of Wales whose popularity and
glory have been evanescent. Not so with the Black Prince.
His glory was not to fade during his life-time or after. Nor his
popularity. He had thirty years of life before him from Crécy
in 1346 to his death in 1376. Whatever vicissitudes of fortune
befell him, Edward the Black Prince was always secure in
the hearts of his countrymen.

No Prince of Wales has ever secured such renown, not at
least while Prince of Wales, though the great Henry V did,
as king, hold as high a repute for his conduct on the battlefield
as ever Edward held.

The Black Prince was the flower of English chivalry so
regarded in his time. His character and life are indeed a
commentary on the qualities which the Middle Ages regarded

as of the highest value in a man of the world. To begin with, the prince was undoubtedly very brave, almost to the point of foolhardiness. He took enormous risks in the field; at Poitiers, for example, he ran the imminent risk of being killed, or at least captured. Then he loved all those feats of arms, in jest as well as earnest, which were the joy of the knights of the age. From boyhood he had loved tournaments and the roughest of knocks in mock fight, so that he was well fitted to be a soldier when his time came.

He could be generous to his opponents. After Poitiers, when he had captured King John of France and his son, Edward waited upon them at table and showed them every courtesy. He treated them as though they were dear friends, and allowed them to sail in their own vessel to England, although he knew that the French were on the watch to try to rescue their king. On the entry into London, the prince rode a small horse while John was on a princely steed.

Then, too, he could be generous to his friends. When, again, after Poitiers, he came upon the sorely wounded Sir John Audley, he gave the latter in recompense of his valiant service substantial rewards in lands and money. He loved splendid entertainments and good living. His court when he was Duke of Aquitaine was one of the most splendid in Europe, and every nobleman and sovereign was eager to visit it, to behold its magnificence and share in it.

His conduct towards Pedro, surnamed the Cruel, of Castile, was extremely, if not foolishly, good-hearted. He did everything for this ungrateful king, supported him when in exile, and used every exertion to put him back on his throne. He poured out money, lives and toil for this end, and it is not too much to say that he gave ultimately his own life for this purpose. After his Spanish campaign he was never the same man.

With all these qualities which are popularly associated with the idea of Christian knighthood it was natural for the prince to take a prominent part in the founding of the Garter, which came in 1348. This Order, now as then one of the most renowned in the whole world, was founded by Edward III as one of the chief manifestations of his love of knighthood. Edward was, in 1348, at the pinnacle of his military glory. He had vanquished the French at Crécy, and his army in England had beaten the Scots at Neville's Cross and taken their king prisoner. He had secured mastery of the narrow seas, and captured Calais, which was to add to his control of the Channel and to serve as a useful base for action against France.

In 1347 and 1348 tournaments on a great scale were held at Windsor, Edward III's birthplace, and foreign knights came from all over Europe to joust at them. The Order of the Blue Garter, under the patronage of St. George, the patron saint of England, was founded and the names of the first knights are a roll of English chivalry. The first name is that of the Black Prince. He, as Prince of Wales, was the obvious choice of a knight for the new Order, and from that time each Prince of Wales automatically becomes a K.G.

Edward III had played with the idea of making the patron of the Order the great hero of legend, King Arthur. The stories of the Knights of the Round Table owed much to the influences of the medieval chivalry. To found another Round Table which should become as famous and noble as that of the mythical Arthur was the king's aim.

After the Order had been founded the king and his companion knights showed how well they understood the nature of chivalry. There was an encounter near Calais with a great French champion, Eustace de Ribemont, in which Edward played rather the part of a knight-errant than of a soldier. In 1350 there was the incident of the sea battle (Les Espagnols sur la mer) with the Spanish pirates, as they might be termed, who had been plundering the coast of England. They suffered a heavy defeat after a terrible encounter in which the highest qualities of courage were shown by king, prince and all their knights.

In addition to these manly and noble qualities which have been illustrated, the prince had other excellencies to round off the medieval conception of a great gentleman. He was graceful in person, skilled in all the accomplishments of peace as well as of war, and well versed in administration. He tried during his rule in Aquitaine to develop trade in the towns under his rule. His name frequently occurs in connection with trade and law-making matters, which at first sight one hardly associates with the brave knight of Crécy.

Then, of course, the prince was devout. So firmly had the Church taken a grip on society that most people pretended to some devotion, if they did not really feel it. Sometimes in the Middle Ages one comes across hardened atheists, but they were usually men of evil life, whose consciences took little or no account of God or man. The Black Prince, on the other hand, appears to have been genuinely pious and to have prayed especially to the Holy Trinity, the Virgin Mary and the saints. Before the battle of Najera or Navarette, as it is variously called, the prince prayed thus:

"Very God, Jesu Christ, who hath formed and created me, consent by your benign grace that I may have this day victory of mine enemies as that I do is in a rightful quarrel to sustain and to aid this king chased out of his own heritage, the which giveth me courage to advance myself to re-establish him again into his realm."

The prince's death-bed scene was one in which the dying man prayed devoutly and then was prevailed upon by his spiritual advisers fully to forgive his enemies.

With all these good qualities, it seems unkind to point out the reverse of the medal. Unfortunately, when the Middle Ages described a man as brave, generous, forgiving, of courtesy and gentleness of heart, they usually meant towards men and women of his own class. Two incidents may illustrate the other side of the prince's character. In 1350 or 1351 the prince rode to subdue some of his men in the Chester territories who had rebelled against his overlordship. He went in arms and took with him a judge in order to hang those who resisted or surrendered to mercy. Then towards the close of his life comes the episode of the capture of Limoges, when in his rage he swore that he would pardon none in the city. He kept this dreadful promise though lying on a litter to watch the slaughter, until he saw three French knights bravely, though hopelessly, resisting. At such a sight the prince's love of manhood and soldierly bravery asserted itself, and he rescinded his order.

The prince's brilliance was purchased at a great cost. He had to get the money somewhere, and this could only be by taxes which must have been wrung from the poorer classes. Generosity of spirit did not extend to the bulk of the labourers and underlings. Their feelings may be gauged by the terrible outbursts which came in France with the Jacquerie and in England with the Peasants' Revolt. The whole pyramid of the social structure of the Middle Ages—King, Lords, Church and Gentry—rested on the broad base of a long-suffering peasantry. The bulk of the taxes were paid by those who had the least wealth.

By a curious feature of literature in the fourteenth century in England, we are able to judge the contrasting outlook on life of the upper and the lower strata of society. In Chaucer's works we see something of the glitter and the glory of Edward's court, or of similar courts of nobles and kings. In *Piers Plowman* we have the life of the poor wretches who had to find the necessary funds for all the beauty of life in the medieval period. There is a remarkable difference in outlook, although strange to say not even in *Piers Plowman* does there seem to be dissatisfaction with the conquests in France. It is even suggested that the Commons will grant such taxes to the king as to enable him to conquer France, if only certain grievances of the poor are redressed.

There is a paradox here. The enormous amount of money spent on maintaining the chivalry of England and the cruel and wicked wars in France would have sufficed to develop a more prosperous state more quickly. A prosperous state did come, in spite of all the waste, but it did not secure the fostering care of the Crown until the times of the Tudor dynasty. These wise sovereigns, whatever their personal foibles or extravagances, did not involve their country in huge foreign wars, but rather did everything in their power to develop trade, commerce and "plantations". This was a complete reversal of the attitude of the Crown in Plantagenet times.

The prince must not be judged too much by standards of a latter day. He did epitomise the ideal of chivalry, as understood in the Middle Ages. Any criticisms of him must be made in the light of that ideal. But nothing can excuse his occasional cruelties or callous treatment of those beneath him.

The prince's sexual life is not without interest. He was a full man and of manly vigour. He was known early in life as a gallant wencher. Two of his bastard sons (there may have been others) are known. One was called Sir John Soltier or

Sounder, of whom Froissart makes mention (vol. i, ch. 393) in connection with some mercenary soldiers who went to Portugal to aid the king against the Spaniards. His motto was "Friends to God, and enemies to all the world". He was hailed by the soldiers as "A Soltier, A Soltier! The valiant bastard" What happened to this bastard of the prince we do not know, but as some English families settled in Portugal he may have left his descendants there. Another bastard of the Black Prince was Sir Roger de Claringdon or Clarendon. He is said by some historians to have founded a family of Smith in Essex, by others to have been the ancestor of the Clarendons. We shall never know, but we do know that Sir Roger de Clarendon was beheaded under Henry IV for asserting that Richard II, Clarendon's half-brother, was alive.

The prince's marriage was with his cousin, Joan, popularly known as the Fair Maid of Kent. She was the daughter of Edmund of Woodstock, Earl of Kent. The latter was a son of Edward I by his second marriage. Joan was married to Thomas, Lord Holland, but after his death rumour and popular opinion were busy in providing her with a second husband. To the prince, it is said, she confessed that her love was for one man, and when he pressed her on the subject she confided to him that he was the one.

There were supposed to be oppositions within the prince's family to the marriage. Edward III was supposed to have wanted a more illustrious alliance for a prince who was the envy of all Europe. The Queen Philippa was said not to be too impressed with her future daughter-in-law's character. Whatever the facts may have been about this parental displeasure, the couple were married, and set up their own household. They seem, as far as one can judge in such matters, to have been very happy. Both had the same tastes in matters of splendid entertaining and appointments, which would naturally be a source of strength to the marriage.

After the prince had been married for some little time it was felt that he and his consort should go to Aquitaine, there to hold the reins of government and rule in his father's place. So to Aquitaine went Edward and Joan, with a splendid train, and set up their magnificent court there. Edward's government appears to have been just and sound, but it must also have been very expensive to support, if the cost of his household and its entertainments are taken into account.

While in France, two sons were born of the marriage. They were Edward of Angouleme, who lived eight years, and Richard of Bordeaux, who was born at Bordeaux in 1366. This was just before the prince's expedition into Spain. It was nothing unusual for foreign kings to visit and even to sojourn at Edward's court. At the time when his son Richard was born, there were residing there James, King of Minorca, and Charles, King of Navarre. They waited for Richard's christening. Then came a king in exile. This was Pedro the Cruel, King of Castile, who had been dethroned by the influence of the French; the latter had set up in his place Pedro's illegitimate half-brother, Don Enrique, or Henry of Trastamera.

The cunning Pedro had correctly gauged the prince's character. He knew that to appear as a suppliant, in the guise of exiled and unjustly dethroned royalty, was to stir in Edward chords which must inevitably act in his favour.

To restore the rightful heir to the throne of his fathers, to exercise the great virtue of justice, this was an aim worthy of the prince's effort, and he listened eagerly to Pedro's version of his sufferings. Nor, after the first flush of indignation on behalf of the unfortunate Pedro, could the prince be blind to the fact that the enemies of his country were active in Spain. It was the French who were the power behind the usurping Henry's throne. So here was a quarrel in which piety, justice and self-interest all combined to urge the prince to make great exertions to place the banner of England south of the Pyrenees.

It was resolved to restore Pedro to his throne. The only question was: how was the money to be found? Still, if money cannot be found for worthwhile purposes, it has always been possible to find it in the cause of war. There was never much ready money available in the Middle Ages, so movables such as jewels and plate were forthcoming, to be converted into money or to serve as pledges for the advancement of loans. Pedro was prodigal with his promises to his "dear brother Edward". According to the terms agreed between the two leaders, certain fortresses in the north of Spain were to be ceded to England, which would help the English cause in France. Large sums of money were advanced to Pedro which he agreed in written bond to repay. In short, nothing was left undone which would enable the prince, with Pedro at his side, to advance across the Pyrenees.

It was in January 1367 that the English army crossed the mountains, and set about the serious task of defeating Don Enrique. The Castilians had help from the French, and large numbers are mentioned as being engaged on the Spanish side—100,000 men, Spaniards, French and mercenaries are quoted, though these numbers are the usual medieval exaggeration. With their experience to guide them, the French counselled their hosts not to fight with the English in the open battlefield, but to wage a guerilla warfare of ambushes and traps. However, it was all in vain, for the prince succeeded in forcing his opponents to meet him in the plains of Castile.

It was at Najera, or Navarette as it is sometimes called, that the armies met. While the enormous numbers quoted cannot be accepted, there is no doubt that, as in all his battles, the prince was outnumbered. The issue of the battle was not at once clear, but when Don Enrique, and the renowned French champion Du Guesclin came against the prince's own line they were discomfited. Don Enrique escaped, but Du Guesclin was captured and treated with all courtesy, as befitted a gallant knight.

It was after the victory that the prince's real troubles began. Don Pedro appears to have had no intention of keeping his word about the large sums which he had borrowed. He turned on his benefactor, and tried to deprive him of his material rewards and of martial glory also.

The prince stayed on in Spain until the autumn of 1367, but then returned with a depleted army to Gascony. His health had broken. He was never the same man again, and it was probably dysentery which laid its foul paw upon him. His health steadily deteriorated.

With his money gone and his health a wreck, the prince was an object of joy to his foes. They had waited twenty years to humble the hero of Crécy, and now was their chance. They began to close in around him.

For his part the prince strove spasmodically but fiercely to hold his ground. The King of France, taking heart from the prince's predicament, sent him a message to come to Paris to render him homage. By the Treaty of Bretigny in 1361 it had been agreed that Aquitaine and the other English territories in the south of France should be free of the necessity of rendering homage to the French king. But now that Edward the king was stricken by premature old age, and Edward the prince laid low by illness, the French king saw his chance and denounced the clauses of the Treaty which abolished the overlordship of France.

The prince responded fiercely to the insolent French demand. "I will come, but with 60,000 men at my back." Alas, his health no longer permitted any but gentle exercise. He could not take the field and had to listen to tales of battles lost and cities retaken by his foes. At last, the revolt of Limoges nerved the prince to greater endeavours. He had himself borne on a litter, and directed the operations from his couch. The massacre of Limoges would have been far worse but for the conduct of the three French knights whom I have already mentioned.

The prince came home to die. Indeed he died a year before his father, who had fallen into a dotage and could not give his full attention to affairs of state.

One of the prince's own sons had died, and the heir to the throne after the prince himself was his elder surviving son, Richard of Bordeaux. He was the third Prince of Wales, and as a century had passed since the institution of the title, it will be of value to look back for a while and to see what conclusions can be drawn so far.

CHAPTER V

Richard of Bordeaux and Henry of Monmouth

AFTER the death of the Black Prince the old king, who was about to celebrate the jubilee of his accession to the throne, was sadly stricken, but not so stricken that he could not attend to urgent matters.

The prince before he died had urged that his surviving son, Richard, should be created Prince of Wales as soon as possible. He was accordingly granted by his grandfather all the titles, possessions and honours of his late father, the prince.

The Commons had made a petition to the king that Richard should be declared heir to the throne and given the title of Prince of Wales. They were answered that the creation and grant of this title was in the king's grant and that he would exercise it when he felt inclined.

Accordingly, the appropriate day having come, Richard was created Prince of Wales, at the age of ten. He was thus to have a long minority, and to be in the hands of powerful relatives and barons. His story is a sad one, for he did many good things but lacked just that additional cement of character which makes a strong man.

Richard II, as he is portrayed for us by Shakespeare, is a man cast in a too meditative mood and turn of mind. He loves peace but his barons long only for war. He cares for the arts of peace, and it is not for nothing that the earliest portrait of an English king painted from an original and of artistic quality is of him (in Westminster Abbey). Richard encouraged art and spent large sums of money on Westminster Abbey and Westminster Hall.

In all probability the secret of the tragedy of Richard II was that he was not sufficiently warlike for his nobles. Richard, like Edward I, confined his attention to the British Isles. He was the first reigning sovereign after Henry II to visit Ireland, and much of his government was good. He maintained a truce with France, and, indeed, married the daughter of the French king. Such a reign gave no chance of plunder to the nobles, and it was this which lay at the bottom of the plots against Richard, and which eventually led to his downfall at the hands of his own cousin.

It was a fact that the long wars with France were popular with the bulk of the people. Far from wearying of the struggles, the ordinary folk were often delighted at the prospect of war with the French. The archers and men at arms returned from the French wars with loads of plunder with which they were able to better their condition. Often they bought farms on which they had worked as boys. Of course many did not return, but human life was then much more liable to an early end than now, and disease, sudden illness, accidents and feuds carried off such large numbers that the loss of a few thousands in war made very little impression upon the survivors.

When the plague visited a country in medieval Europe the inhabitants were virtually defenceless against it. The Black Death reduced the population of England, which was then (1348) reckoned at about 4,000,000, by half. The Black Death was probably a form of bubonic plague and may well have been carried from as far away as China by the itinerant merchants who traded across Europe and Asia until the savage Mongols made the routes too unsafe. Students of medicine must derive considerable interest from studying the records of great pestilences. Literature contains many cases of famous plagues which arose and afflicted mankind almost without check. Thucydides records the plague of Athens in the time of Pericles (fourth century B.C.); we have just mentioned the visitation of Edward III's time, and then the Plague of 1665 will occur to everyone's mind.

We now know the causes of most of these terrible disasters, and would know how to prevent them, but our ancestors could only accept them as the will of heaven. Only persons of robust constitution survived.

The outlook of Richard II's subjects was callous on the matter of death and suffering. Though we have witnessed horrible events in the twentieth century, we know that these things are a retrogression from a better condition. To the folk of 1377–99, their conditions as regards suffering were normal. They therefore blamed the king for his lack of ability in making successful war on France. Had he invaded France and conquered Normandy he could have demanded huge sums from his parliaments and got them. But because he tried to set up some organisation in Ireland and kept England at peace he was unpopular. Instead of using the great nobles, his kinsmen, he gave his confidence to men of lower degree who were able administrators and who looked to him alone. Unpardonable crime! Bushy, Bagot, Green, the men whom Shakespeare (following the chroniclers) placed around Richard, stank in the nostrils of the great ones of England.

By the time of Richard of Bordeaux the sage scheme of William the Conqueror to keep his nobles dependent had worked out rather badly. In 1086 there were round about 180 tenants-in-chief of the Crown. By three hundred years later, only some fifty great men ranked among the prime nobility. The cause of the frightful civil wars of the next century, known as the Wars of the Roses, was really at root the close relationship existing between the nobles. The term "cousin" which is still formally used in communications between the sovereign and the dukes, is derived from the fact that in the fourteenth and fifteenth centuries the nobles of the highest rank were indeed cousins of the sovereign.

Consequently Richard II had a difficult task before him. At one stage he saw his friends driven from his side and murdered or exiled. Naturally this led to a bitter hatred on the king's part for some of his nobles. In 1397 the king arrested his uncle, the Duke of Gloucester, and of the other nobles, the Earls of Arundel and Warwick. Gloucester was murdered in Calais by Richard's orders. Soon Arundel was condemned and executed, while the Archbishop of Canterbury was sent into exile. Richard's capricious nature then showed itself. Those noblemen who had supported him, the Dukes of Norfolk and Hereford, were through various devious ways driven into disputes and exiled. Hereford was the king's first cousin and was the eldest son of John of Gaunt.

This was in September 1398, and in the following May Richard was so sure of himself that he went again to Ireland. While he was there Hereford landed in Yorkshire in July 1399. In the meantime John of Gaunt had died, and Hereford (or Henry of Bolingbroke, as he is often called) announced when he appeared in England that he came merely to seek his own. He knew, of course, that he had many supporters awaiting him in England, and as he received fresh strength his pretensions grew. Richard hurried back from Ireland and landed in Wales. He was forced to surrender to Henry at Flint, and from then on it was a matter of time until he was forced into abdication.

In February 1400 Richard died in the Castle of Pontefract, where he had been closely immured following the signature by him of his instrument of abdication. In the Shakespearean story he dies by violence, but some think his constitution could not stand the rigours of the confinement in winter. His removal, from whatever cause, must have been gratifying to Henry IV, as Bolingbroke was now known, but it soon proved anything but favourable. The new king had gained the throne by revolting against the lawful king, and by the help of men whose faith had been plighted to Richard. Treason soon breeds treason, and Henry found his tenure of the throne a hard task. He had several rebellions to put down, notably that of the Percies of Northumberland. He had to contend with a recrudescence of the Welsh national spirit. Owen Glendower raised the revolt in Wales. The Welsh had been fond of Richard and they did not take kindly to his successor and supplanter. Throughout the whole of Henry IV's reign Wales was in strife and turmoil. Then Glendower died and his power fell with him.

The succession to the throne of Henry IV brought with it a call to high dignity for a youth who had never expected it. This was Henry or Harry of Monmouth, the eldest son of

Henry IV. He was to be the fourth Prince of Wales. When he was born, he was, though of royal and noble birth, not in succession to the throne, and his education was therefore that of a noble's son, without question of training for royal responsibilities. It may be added that as heir to the vast possessions of John of Gaunt, young Henry would from an early age be accustomed to responsibility of a high order.

He was instructed in music and in books of grammar and, of course, in military exercises. His father seems not to have taken much interest in his eldest son, apart from the fact that he was travelling some of the time of Henry's boyhood in various parts of Europe and Asia. Curiously enough, Henry's education owed much to the care of his royal cousin, Richard II. The latter during his brief tenure of supreme power altered the terms of Bolingbroke's exile more than once. Finally Richard confiscated all the property of the exiled future Henry IV. He then took under his care young Harry of Monmouth. Harry was in fact a sort of prisoner; there was definite restraint on his movements. "The boy prisoner was narrowly watched, and yet notwithstanding the terms on which King and Lord mutually stood—oppressor and oppressed, the captive and the gaoler learned to love each other; and Richard settled on his cousin £500 a year, which was after all not excessively liberal, seeing that he had plundered Henry's father of a thousandfold that amount." So wrote Dr. Doran in *Princes of Wales*.

When Richard set out on his second and fatal Irish expedition he took Harry with him. He expended certain sums on coat armour for the young warrior. The royal forces landed at Waterford, and advanced against one of the Irish chieftains, Mac Murchard. It was in June 1399 that Harry of Monmouth first saw warfare, in the wilds of Ireland. Harry was then able to witness grim fighting. The Irish, confident in the wild nature of their west country, decided to await Richard's coming in some woods. Richard decided to burn them out. Many Irish villages were destroyed and much land, naturally undernourished, was devastated completely. In the light of camp fires Harry of Monmouth was dubbed knight. He was not yet twelve years of age. He accompanied Richard in the march to Dublin, and then he learned that his father had decided to make himself King of England.

Richard, when he set out for England, left Henry behind in Trym Castle. They parted with expressions of regret and mutual assurances that Henry was innocent of any participation in his father's revolt against Richard. Was there not perhaps something of reminiscence of these pleasant exchanges in Henry's mind when some fourteen years later he had the body of Richard removed from its humble tomb at King's Langley and buried again with proper ceremony and care at Westminster?

Henry IV was crowned on 13th October 1399, only a fortnight after his cousin Richard had renounced the throne. On 15th October 1399 Henry of Monmouth was created Prince of Wales, being then only two months past twelve years.

The creation of the fourth prince was made at the request of the Commons, though it would have taken place without their request. Henry IV was willy-nilly compelled to be a constitutional sovereign, and he therefore returned a conciliatory answer to the Commons. He affected to consult them, and it was then said that, by the consent of all the estates of the realm, Henry of Monmouth was made Prince of Wales, and invested with the titles of Duke of Cornwall, Aquitaine, Lancaster, and Earl of Chester.

It was in Westminster Hall that the Prince of Wales was brought to receive from the hands of his father the gold coronet adorned with pearls, the ring and the rod of office.

From then on commenced the career of the great conqueror whom we call Henry V. Rapidly did the youth learn his trade. Apt pupil he must have been, for he was only thirteen when he went to Scotland to meet his father's enemies. In Ireland when he was twelve, in Scotland at thirteen, and in Wales at fourteen, the young prince was swiftly learning all the practical dispositions of war. No more tournament training for him, but a real apprenticeship to the trade of fighting.

Apart from war, the Prince of Wales was a lover of field sports, hunting, hawking, fishing, riding and walking. He was fleet of foot and able with his lords to outrun a deer and capture it. He was far from unskilled in mental studies also. He was well educated and pious, being particularly attached to the services of the Church. Altogether he seems to have been a serious hardworking youth and ever ready to learn.

He warred in Wales against Glendower. It was not, however, until 1403, when he was fourteen, that Henry was involved in a pitched battle of the full medieval kind. At Shrewsbury battle was joined with Hotspur, the son of the Earl of Northumberland and the leader of the Percies. Long and bitterly was the battle contested, and it was finally decided by a furious charge made by Hotspur against the royal army. To slay Henry IV was the great object of the rebels. Knowing this, the king had dressed several gentlemen in his coat of arms and four of these had been killed by Hotspur or Douglas, the former's confederate. Hotspur, when he charged the royal line for the last time, tried to reach the king himself, but at last an arrow pierced his head and he fell from his horse lifeless. The death of Hotspur took the nerve from his followers. They gave way in all directions and the battle and the crown were won for Henry IV, and the future Henry V.

In that last fierce struggle Henry of Monmouth received his first wound, an arrow in the face. He was fully blooded that day, and made a warrior. He acquitted himself gallantly and there could be no doubt that his father had a worthy successor.

It was the great first Duke of Marlborough who said that he read only Shakespeare for his English history. Generally, Shakespeare is a sound guide, but this prince of poets has not scrupled to set down as historic fact what is only poetic fancy. What should have happened does not always happen. In the case of Henry of Monmouth, no one can ever forget the change which came over him when he (in Shakespeare's play, that is) decides to abandon his low companions and to be himself.

This picture of the dissolute Prince of Wales, obsessed with drink, women and low company, brawls and fights, is one always in the mind when Henry V is mentioned. Likewise there is the story of his affray with Judge Gascoigne. The judge had sentenced to prison a servant of the prince. Enraged by this, the prince appeared in the court and demanded the release of his servant. Not obtaining his demand, he is said to have struck the judge, who then promptly sentenced him to prison.

It makes a wonderfully good story, but it does not accord with the character of the prince as shown, not only in his reign, but in his youth. His youth was strenuous and serious, laborious, with little time for the follies with which the first part of Shakespeare's Henry IV is filled.

The story about Henry and Judge Gascoigne does not appear until more than a century after Henry's death—it is related by Sir Thomas Elyot in 1531. The only possible period in the prince's life when the stories of dissipation and unruliness could have been true is in the years 1411–1413, when the prince had been dismissed from the Council.

In truth, the Prince of Wales was too successful in his schooling. He was put to the Welsh wars in earnest after the fall of Hotspur had deprived Owen Glendower of his strongest supporter in England. The reign of Henry IV continued to be troubled; there was still trouble with Hotspur's father, the Earl of Northumberland; the Scots were, as usual, causing havoc along the border, and the Welsh revolt burnt like a strong but wayward fire. In the north the rebellious lords were put down. In Wales not only had the prince to contend against great difficulties of terrain, and of actual warfare, but he had the constant embarrassment of lack of money to pay his troops.

When first he went into the Welsh wars the prince had been forced to pawn what valuables he possessed to pay his men. After Shrewsbury, the king made over to him the plate belonging to the prisoners taken in the battle. This relieved the prince's distress for the time, but again in 1405 he was forced to pawn plate and jewels.

Yet despite all this the prince made headway, and by 1407–8 he had reconquered Wales, and Owen Glendower sank into an obscurity so profound that not even his grave is accurately known. Then the prince was sent to Scotland to deal with troubles there. In Scotland also he was brilliantly successful, and so on his return to London he was not unnaturally one of the Great Council (the Privy Council, that is) of the realm. He was not only a member of the Council but President of it;

Captain of Calais, and Warden of the Cinque Ports. There was no aspect of government as understood in the fourteenth and fifteenth centuries into which he did not penetrate. He helped to clear the Channel of pirates; he corresponded with the great potentates of the time, the Pope or the Emperor, the Duke of Burgundy, etc., as though he were almost the head of the state.

No doubt the ill-health of Henry IV, which grew ever worse, was one cause of the prince being so prominently employed, but, unlike some of his predecessors in the principality, he had the necessary ability to govern and to lead. It was the astonishing progress he had made which awakened his father's jealousy.

Henry IV knew only too well the secrets of conspiracy, and how he had overturned the throne of Richard II. He lived in dread of further plots, and even his own son was not free from suspicion. Henry may have been a leper, and was in any event a very sick man. No doubt the prince had tasted to the full the sweets of power and longed to be absolute. This is no doubt the germ of the Shakespearean story that he took the Crown to wear it while his father lay asleep. He certainly did at one time suggest that his father should retire or abdicate in his favour.

The king's answer was to remove his son from the Council. This was the condition of things from 1411 to the king's death in 1413. It could be that during this time the prince, in the desperation of a strong nature baulked of its natural food, found relief in dissipation. It could be, but there is no evidence to show that it was so. The nature of the man seems far removed from it. For one thing, Henry of Monmouth was a very religious man—religious according to the ideas of the fifteenth century. There is one instance of his presence at the execution of a tailor named John Badby. The latter had been found guilty of failing to believe in transubstantiation, and for this was condemned to be burnt alive. Burning was a new punishment in England, and was brought into the calendar of the law by the clergy.

Henry IV, having an insecure tenure of the throne, was forced to listen very carefully to the wishes of his Parliament.

The clerical side of Parliament was anxious to root out the incipient Protestants, known as Lollards. Under the power of Henry IV's father the great reformer John Wycliff had lived and had died in his bed. Henry IV had to bend his way to the wishes of the great ecclesiastics. They knew that the only way to combat heresy was by force. The hateful law, *De Heretico Comburendo*, was passed in 1401, and under this law for the first time in England a man could be punished for his opinions. Punished by death by burning.

Prince Henry was present at the execution of Badby and used every means in his power to bring the condemned man to a recantation of his heresy, but it was useless, so the prince had to leave him to the flames. The prince had done what he conceived his best to save the man but was not prepared in the name of humanity to go against the ecclesiastical law. Then, again, after he had succeeded to the throne the new king, Henry V, had to deal with a worse Lollard outbreak, the leader of which, Sir John Oldcastle, was a great friend of his own in his youth. Oldcastle had shared the rigours of the Welsh campaign. He seemed to set himself at the head of a large Lollard conspiracy. It was put down by the force of Henry V and his prompt action. Oldcastle was captured and eventually burnt as a heretic. It is possible to excuse his death as that of a rebel.

We see, then, in Henry of Monmouth a Prince of Wales who has been prepared in the most thorough manner for his work as king. When he succeeds to the throne he shows how well he has learnt the lessons given to him. In 1413 Henry V was only twenty-five. He soon advanced a claim to the throne of France as his great-grandfather Edward III had done in 1340.

To the French the recurrence of this English claim must have seemed the most terrible scourge their beautiful country had ever had to meet. They had not been fortunate in their sovereigns during the Hundred Years War, and at the time of Henry's succession to the English throne the French king was the mad Charles VI, whose son, the Dauphin, was a weak-seeming youth, whom no one took seriously.

Henry may well have thought, in addition, that to make war on France would prevent his knights from plotting at home.

There were probably several motives mixed in Henry's mind: the desire to win the French throne and ambition to win personal glory, as well as the need to keep his own subjects occupied.

However the situation was brought about, there could be no question that Henry pursued his aims with great skill and care. Of the conquests of Edward III and the former English possession in France he held only Calais. To augment this, he skilfully laid siege to Harfleur at the mouth of the Seine. This he captured and then set out to march towards Calais. Near Agincourt his way was barred by an army several times larger than his own. The immortal story of his victory has been told so many times that one need only glance at it. Agincourt was not only a most valiant battle of the few against the many, but also a very skilful combat on the English side. Henry's dispositions were very well made, and his army placed to the best advantage, and it was, in fact, his force which soon took the initiative, a quality in which the French commanders were sadly lacking.

After Agincourt Henry set himself to build up his position in France. He subdued Normandy. He cleared the Channel of piratical and French shipping. He used the weapons of diplomacy to bring the Emperor Sigismund round to his side. The emperor was a not very effective ruler, and when he tried to intervene in the Anglo-French war he found himself treated with courtesy, but that was all.

The settlement of the long schism of the Church and the election of Pope Martin V owed something to Henry's intervention. All this, combined with his victories over the French, gave him a great position in Europe. He was on the way to the headship of Christendom. In 1420 he concluded peace with the French in a treaty which sounds incredible. By it (the Treaty of Troyes) he was acknowledged by the French king as his heir, while the Dauphin was cast out as a bastard; in addition, the French king bestowed on Henry his daughter Catherine as his bride.

Henry V had achieved in his short reign far more than any other English warrior against France. The dream of one realm of England and France seemed on the point of being realized, and it was clear that the king of such a vast realm would be the equal or more of the Holy Roman Emperor. In fact, Henry decided that it was time for him to think of going on Crusade. When he lay dying he declared that had he been spared he would, after settling the affairs of France, have gone on pilgrimage to Palestine with an army and have freed the Holy Land from the Turks.

Death cut short the great schemes of Henry V. His infant son, Henry VI, was, indeed, crowned King of England and of France, but he lost both.

Henry V died in 1422. He was fortunate not to have outlived his glory. More than a century had passed since, in 1302, the title of Prince of Wales was first used for the heir to the throne of England. During the one hundred and twenty years from 1302 to 1422 four Princes of Wales were created: Edward II, the Black Prince, Richard II and Henry V.

In these four princes we have the means of studying the institution, if such term may be used, of the Prince of Wales as heir to the throne. What conclusions can be drawn as to age, power of conferment, and means of education from these four cases?

In the first place, the matter of age remains as it has been ever since, very doubtful and full of conjecture, which the recent creation of Prince Charles has done nothing to alter. Setting aside the story of the infant prince in arms, we see that Edward of Caernarvon was declared Prince of Wales at the age of seventeen. The Black Prince was thirteen; Richard II was only ten (there was, however, a special reason for this, because the king, his grandfather, did not expect to live long); Henry V was twelve when created Prince of Wales. The probable conclusion is that just about the age of entering into the teens is the more usual time for the creation of a Prince of Wales.

With regard to the power of conferment, it is quite clear that the sovereign's prerogative is exercised in the creation of his or her son as Prince of Wales. Despite the apparent precedent of the Black Prince (created with the assent of all the great ones of England), it is made very clear in the case of Richard II that the power to create and the decision as to time is not a matter for any minister or Parliament, but for the sovereign alone. So it continues to be.

Another interesting feature is that the sovereign may create his grandson Prince of Wales. This only occurs in the case of a grandson who succeeds as heir apparent to an eldest son. Two cases of this kind have occurred, once after the death of the Black Prince, the other when George II's eldest son died, and when the future George III, grandson of George II, was created Prince of Wales.

What of education? Here we enter on a wide field and deductions can be made which are applicable to the present day.

It must be clear at once that the education of a Prince of Wales was much harder in older days than in our own. Not that the element of hardship has gone out of princely education. Anyone who has read of the education at a naval training college of the present Duke of Windsor will know that.

Nor is the difference between the physical hazards of medieval times and those of today the only mark of distinction which divides the education of a Prince of Wales in 1958 and in 1358, or 1458. The wearing of armour was a general characteristic of medieval warfare, and it was natural for a prince to get early into the habit, hence the small suits of armour such as those at the Tower. The wearing of armour did not go out because of any effeminacy or decline in the royal house. It went simply because firearms and other weapons rendered it less valuable in war. Finally, it became an encumbrance.

There is no reason to suppose that a modern Prince of Wales would be any the less able than his predecessors to endure the labour and stress of medieval fighting, whether in the tilt yard or actual battle. The riding of the Prince of Wales, now Duke of Windsor, was accompanied by a good many hazards, and indeed public opinion considered it too dangerous for the heir to the throne.

No, the real difference in education between the fifteenth century and our own time lies in the fact that the powers of the sovereign are much less than were those of the medieval monarch. It is a truism, but one usually forgotten, that right up to the end of the seventeenth century the country was really ruled by its sovereign. Thus the character of that sovereign mattered enormously. As we shall have occasion to remind ourselves later, the outlook of the king was considered of such importance that James II lost his throne in consequence of his; and his son, the unfortunate Prince of Wales, spent his whole life in exile—again because his views on certain fundamental matters were intolerable to his countrymen.

Thus, since the power and responsibilities of the monarch were so great, then clearly the earlier the education of the heir-apparent were begun the better. Edward the Black Prince was actually in the seat of power before he was created Prince of Wales; that is, when he was not ten. How could a boy of such a tender age, and a natural boy full of high spirits, be wholly engrossed in matters of Parliament, such as the move of the wool staple, or the taxes to be levied for the support of the army in France? Of course he could not. But a boy of any intelligence exposed to such surroundings even for a few hours a week, and for a few weeks a year, would soon have some idea of what was going on. Suppose that the present Prince of Wales, on the occasion when his mother and father pay a state visit to, for example, Canada, were to be called from the society of his school-fellows at Cheam to preside at the meeting of the Estates of the Realm—that is, the Parliament. The boy might find it on the whole very dull; some of the matter would be beyond his comprehension, but he would very quickly gain an idea of what Parliamentary Government was like.

The education of the Prince of Wales is therefore conditioned by the spirit of the times, and especially by the attitude of the age towards monarchy. For the past one hundred and thirty years at least the sovereign has been expected to reign and not rule.

In the period at present under review the prince was educated in the traditional manner of a prince: to govern his future people. The Shakespearean thesis of a madcap Hal, who suddenly reforms, and becomes pious, learned and valiant, is completely contradicted by the fact that the young prince was presiding over the Council, dealing with King and Emperor and Pope, after having led the army and the navy to victory over England's foes. He was removed from the Council, not because Henry IV thought him a useless gallant, but because his father feared the growing power of the prince.

So the training of a Prince of Wales in older days was strenuous in the extreme. Few mistakes were tolerated. This is borne out by the reaction of the advisers of a young prince, especially one who was a minor when he came to the throne. Henry VI, for one example, was early discovered to be, shall we say, simple. This was clearly discovered because he had been tried with affairs of state at an age when his father, Henry of Monmouth, was already a knight, and when tried had been found sadly and ingloriously wanting. Still, he would be king, in fact, when he reached his majority, and therefore something had to be done. He was found a strong wife. Of this more presently.

We can therefore sum up by saying that the right to create a Prince of Wales was clearly the sovereign's own prerogative; the rights of the Parliament were confined to a prayer that the sovereign might graciously be pleased to consider the matter of creating the heir Prince of Wales. When an eldest son died, the king could create that eldest son's son prince in his place. The education of the prince was such, in actual experience, of responsibility, as would fit him to govern his realm.

Of the four Princes whose careers we have reviewed, the first was murdered at the end of his reign; the second died before he could inherit the throne, but after, let it be said, a career of glory which no other Prince of Wales has equalled; the third was deposed from the throne, and probably murdered or driven to die. The fourth succeeded to the throne and reigned gloriously though briefly.

What of the next century, the fifteenth? Within the period of fifty years there were created five others. These were: (1) Edward of Westminster, the Prince of the House of Lancaster, son of Henry VI; (2) Edward of the Sanctuary, Prince of the House of York ; (3) Edward of Middleham, again of York; (4) Arthur of Winchester; and (5) Henry of Greenwich. These were created between 1453 and 1503.

What was their fate? The first was killed after Tewkesbury; the second died in the Tower, as Edward V; the third died mysteriously while still only a boy; the fourth died as a youth;

only the fifth was prosperous, and became that dread sovereign, Henry VIII.

The tale of misfortunes is not complete until the twentieth century, when the most popular of all Princes of Wales succeeded to the throne, only to abdicate within the year.

CHAPTER VI

The Century of Tragedy

FROM 1399, when Henry of Monmouth (Henry V) was created Prince of Wales, until 1502, when Prince Arthur, elder son of Henry VII, died, only one of the Princes of Wales could be described as fortunate. He was the great Harry of Agincourt. For consider the others. The Lancastrian prince, Edward of Westminster or of Lancaster, was slain at or after the battle of Tewkesbury. The next was Edward of York, the elder son of Edward IV, who was also the elder of the princes in the Tower. He did in a sense come to the throne, and always figures among our kings, but no one really knows what happened to him except that it is certain that he came to a violent end. The king who took Edward V's place was Richard III, and he hastened to make his son, Edward of Middleham, the Earl of Salisbury, Prince of Wales. Yet only a few months passed between the boy's creation as prince and his death. Then, last, we have Arthur of Winchester, the elder son of Henry VII. He died before he was sixteen.

Thus out of five Princes of Wales only one reigned; and though that one was glorious, his glory only serves to throw up into greater relief the sad and dismal fates of the other four. It is the purpose of this chapter not only to tell their story but, as throughout the rest of this book, to try to illustrate the times in which these princes lived and the manner in which they were fitted and educated for the throne.

We begin, then, with the period succeeding the death of Henry V. Probably no marriage in the royal annals of England had more of policy and less of romance than that of Henry V and Catherine of France. I think it was the French historian, Michelet, who speaks of Catherine being forced to receive into

her bed the enemy of France, and quite probably the wooing
scene in Shakespeare's *Henry V* is not fanciful. A king like
Henry V, chaste and virtuous, a born leader and ruler, and
a pious man, probably did not possess the qualities which
make a lover. What would have been the outcome of the
union had Henry lived out the normal span is not easy to
conjecture. He died when he was thirty-five. His widow
consoled herself with a friend, one Owen Tudor, and subsequently married him. From this alliance of Catherine and
Tudor came the great House of the Tudors.

It is certain that Henry V would have been very disappointed
in his son, Henry VI, had he lived to see the boy grow up. He
who talked of begetting a boy who should go to Constantinople
and take the Turk by the beard would have felt sadly dis-
illusioned by the apparent weakness of Henry VI. The latter
was one year old when he succeeded his father. At eight he
was crowned King of England and at ten King of France. The
latter ceremony took place in Notre Dame in Paris, and it
is a fact that the only English king ever to be crowned King of
France was the poor soul who never directed a fight in person or
showed any powers of leadership at all. Not William the
Conqueror, or Edward III or Henry V, but Henry VI, was
actually anointed King of France! This ceremony was an
answer to the French revival under Joan of Arc, which led to
the crowning of the Dauphin at Rheims.

The events of Henry's life can be summed up by saying that
he remained on the throne until 1461, when he was deposed
in favour of his cousin Edward IV. He was restored to the
throne by the king-making Earl of Warwick in 1470 and so
nominally reigned until his deposition for the second time in
1471, which was followed by his death, probably by murder.
What was the matter with Henry VI?

His character was amiable; he was a faithful friend and
honest and well-meaning. He had not the strength of character
needed to deal with his barons or with the problems raised by
his father's conquests in France. It is at least arguable
that a man of fairly strong mind could have renewed the
campaigns in France and turned back the tide of French
nationalism after Joan of Arc's death. Henry never showed

any desire to take part in war. His great interests were religion and scholarship. Added to his other troubles, the king had periods which are described as insanity by some writers. He certainly did not know what he was doing during periods varying from weeks to months.

It was early decided by the young king's advisers that he should have a strong partner in marriage. Perhaps it was this which led the Duke of Suffolk (William de la Pole) to seek out Margaret, the daughter of René, the titular King of Sicily and Jerusalem. She was poor and her father, though of royal blood, was of little account, but she was beautiful and determined, of great courage and resolution. It was felt that she might uphold the king's weak will.

Certainly Queen Margaret had a hard life. She was not popular in England because of her French origin, and her husband, although a good and kind man, could not be of much help to her. Soon after their only child, Edward, was born, the king went into one of his strange states of mental absence. Even when the queen brought the infant before the king and besought him to know his child, he remained oblivious of his surroundings. It was not until something like fifteen months had passed, at the Christmas of 1454, that Henry VI came to himself. In the words which an old chronicler attributes to him: "He never knew till that time, nor wist not what was said to him, nor wist not where he had been, whiles he had been sick till now." When he thus recovered, the king inquired about the boy's godparents.

There were many rumours that the boy Edward was not the king's son. It was said, for instance, that when the king, by reason of his mental trouble, could not attend his child's christening, his absence from the church did not imply the absence of the father. There were continual canards and slanders about the queen, and several names were mentioned as possible fathers for her son. Some even said openly that young Edward was a bastard begot in Coventry.

The reason for these scandalous tales seems to have lain in the fact that Edward's birth had disappointed some powerful nobles, and particularly Richard, Duke of York. All goes back to the fact that, of the numerous sons of Edward III, several lived to manhood. His eldest son, the Black Prince, died, as we have seen, before his father, and the Black Prince's line became extinct with Richard II. Edward III's second son, William of Hatfield, died young, but his third son was a great hulking giant, Lionel of Antwerp, Duke of Clarence. Lionel left no male issue, but through his only daughter the Earls of March had the rightful claim to the throne after the extinction of the Black Prince's line.

In 1399 the son of Edward III's fourth son, John of Gaunt, succeeded in pushing Richard II off the throne. Henry IV never had a quiet tenure of the Crown he had ambitiously striven to gain. He kept his cousin of March a prisoner, yet it was through the marriage of a daughter of March with Richard, Earl of Cambridge (son of Edmund, Duke of York, the fifth son of Edward III), that the Yorkist claim to the throne followed.

So far had this claim been recognised that Richard, Duke of York was the heir presumptive to the Crown until the birth of young Edward, and during the king's illness the Duke of York was named as Protector and Defender of the King. It can be imagined with what ill grace the Duke of York and the other partisans of his cause saw the birth of a son to the poor monarch. Not only was the Duke of York the heir presumptive before Edward's birth, but through his descent from Edward III's third son, Lionel, mentioned above, the Duke of York claimed a prior right to the throne over Henry VI himself.

Thus the reason existed to prompt the outcry against the chastity of Queen Margaret and the legitimacy of her son. There is probably no more to be said for these stories than for those which cast doubts on the legitimacy of the young "warming-pan" Prince of Wales two hundred years later.

Still, whatever the truth of these stories, the Yorkist faction were not going to sit down quietly under the rule of the enfeebled Lancastrians. Henry VI's son had been born in 1453, the year in which the English Empire in France finally crashed, after the death of the great Earl Talbot at Chatillon. In 1455 began the first battle of the Wars of the Roses (not so named during the time of conflict). This was the battle of St. Albans.

Henry of Monmouth, Prince of Wales, 1399: afterwards Henry V.

Edward of Westminster Prince of Wales, 1454: Son of Henry VI.

Henry, brother of Arthur, Prince of Wales, 1503: afterwards Henry VIII.

Arthur Tudor, Prince of Wales, 1489: died before his father, Henry VII.

At this the queen's champion, the Duke of Somerset, was defeated and killed, and the Duke of York was supreme.

Edward, the young prince, was created Prince of Wales in his first year, this being the first instance of one so young becoming prince. After the Duke of York had won the battle of St. Albans the Parliament laid down that proper provision was to be made for the prince's upbringing, 10,000 marks being settled on him until he was eight years old, and 16,000 marks from eight to fourteen years old.

The queen, meanwhile, made every effort to make her son's position secure, but perhaps her ambition was over-anxious. At any rate, four years after some sort of peace had been worked out between York and Lancaster the Yorkists went into revolt. They defeated the Lancastrians at Blore Heath and again at Northampton, after which they captured the king and led him to London. There one of those shameful scenes took place which show us the Middle Ages in their true perspective—having as little respect for rights of legitimate government as many countries have in our own century: Henry VI was made to acknowledge Richard of York as his heir, to the exclusion of his own son, Edward.

In fact the Duke of York was actually styled by the ordinance of Parliament Prince of Wales, Duke of Cornwall, and Earl of Chester. He was also termed Protector of England, a title which two hundred years later was thus seen to have a respectable antiquity and precedent.

There were thus two Princes of Wales in the same realm, the only known instance in our history. Who was the real Prince of Wales?

With his mother Edward had fled (he was seven years old) to Durham, thence to Chester and then to Wales. The queen and the prince were robbed of 10,000 marks in jewels and money. From Wales they at length reached Scotland. There the queen received from the Scottish queen assistance for her cause. The King of Scots, James III, was only a boy, and perhaps this fact had something to do with the help rendered to Queen Margaret.

With the aid of Scottish troops the queen invaded England, and at the battle of Wakefield in 1460 the Duke of York was defeated and slain. The queen's triumph was short-lived, for two more battles were fought, one at Mortimer's Cross, the other the second battle of St. Albans. In both of these the Lancastrians were defeated. Yet, even so, the lion-hearted queen fought on and at Barnet Heath drove back the Earl of Warwick, soon to be known as the king-maker. The old King, Henry VI, was reunited with his family and, at the queen's instance, conferred the honour of knighthood on his son. Margaret was not always well advised and allowed her northern troops to pillage the country to the gates of London.

The Londoners stood firm for the son of the dead Duke of York, and he was soon put on the throne as King Edward IV. He was a brave and skilful soldier and within two weeks had routed the Lancastrians at Towton in Yorkshire.

After each battle the victors were in the habit of executing their enemies. No quarter was given to captive nobles. Why was it that the English nobility tore each other to pieces in this fashion?

It is easy to say that the nobility of England had become a kind of closed shop. When the Conqueror had parcelled out the lands of England among his Norman followers he had been careful to divide the lands of his great barons. Consequently, there were about 180 great tenants of the Crown, with lands distributed all over England. Naturally the nobles did not care for this arrangement and strove to make things better from their own point of view by amalgamation of estates and families. By the time of the Wars of the Roses, four hundred years after William the Conqueror's time, there were some forty great lords who held most of the estates of the great tenants in chief. The king-maker himself held four earldoms.

Moreover, through the numerous children of Edward III, and the marriages between the royal house and the nobility, most of the great peers were connected by blood or marriage with the royal family. The dukedoms were royal, which is the reason for the mode of formal address used by the Crown in writing to a duke now. "Cousin" meant literally cousin between a duke and the king in the Middle Ages.

There was, therefore, the hostility which sometimes arises among relatives. Yet this will not account for all the horrors of the Civil War. At the back of the trouble was the fact that with the end of the French war great numbers of ex-servicemen were thrown on to the country without adequate means of support. Their sole trade was war and they soon found that the only way they could live was by attaching themselves to the household of some great noble. Consequently there were always a large number of men ready to fight out a quarrel whether it were against the law or for it. These retainers gave the great lords a feeling of confidence in their ability to use force. It was quite easy for quarrels to break out into violence and so to war.

Once the quarrels were being decided by battle, restraint was thrown to the winds. The whole of society went back, and anarchy often threatened the nation. At the end of the Wars of the Roses society had changed drastically and, as a result, an entirely new order came into being.

To return to the story of Edward, Prince of Wales. With his parents he found refuge in Scotland, where the king was driven to pawn Berwick-on-Tweed to the Scots king in order to secure assistance. There followed a series of wretched wanderings during which the queen with the prince was once at the mercy of a robber in Hexham Forest, who proved more amenable to gentle entreaty than the Yorkist lords, and who did all in his power to protect the young Prince of Wales.

At last, after many wanderings, the queen and the prince reached the Continent and the court of the Duke of Burgundy. He, although a friend of Edward IV, did not refuse to succour the fugitives and eventually allowed them to go on their way to the domains of Rene, Margaret's father. Here for some years there was peace while the Prince of Wales was able to study and to learn something of the duties of his office. He had already learnt a great deal about the instability of princes, the dangers which surround a throne and other common themes of the moralist.

When Edward reached Europe he was not more than ten years old, and yet he had been through more vicissitudes than many a hardened soldier of adult years. In the few years of peace left to him he was to study under the best masters whom his mother could afford. Among his tutors was Sir John Fortescue, whose treatise on the laws of England was written with the primary object of instructing the prince in the laws of the land he was to govern. Nor were martial exercises overlooked. Too well did Margaret and Edward know that his throne would be won only by hard fighting.

Curiously enough, the turn of fate which gave Edward a chance came through the arch enemy of Lancaster, Warwick. That gentleman had not been successful in managing Edward IV, as he had expected to do. The young king had proved unexpectedly obstinate over the subject of marriage. Worse still, he had made Warwick look foolish, for the latter had negotiated a marriage with the sister of the French king. To his amazement and indignation Warwick found that the king who was to make this politic union with the French king's sister was already married to Lady Elizabeth Woodville.

This event naturally poisoned the feelings of Warwick. There were plots and counterplots. Edward became for a time the prisoner of Warwick, escaped, left England, then returned and forced Warwick to flee. As a result, Warwick repaired to the court of France, and became the ally of Margaret. Warwick's daughter, Anne Neville, was to marry the Prince of Wales. In fact at the age of seventeen the prince was married or at least betrothed to the Lady Anne. On the strength of Warwick's support the queen and prince landed in England. Warwick went in advance of the queen, to his overthrow at Barnet at the hands of Edward IV, a brilliant soldier as well as hardy fighter.

Margaret and Edward went on with another army to meet the conqueror of Warwick, and meet him they did at Tewkesbury, where the Lancastrian cause went down into utter ruin. Whatever may have happened earlier—and some would have us believe in the Prince of Wales fighting when he was barely ten years old—certainly at Tewkesbury Edward, Prince of Wales, fought bravely as a leader. Dr. Doran says: "Margaret repeatedly urged his extreme youth, but the Black Prince was younger when he won Cressy. She spoke of his inexperience, but this boy of girlish beauty had at least seen more fields than

Henry of Monmouth when the latter was entrusted with the conduct of the war in Wales.''

How Edward died is disputed. Some say that he fell bravely fighting in the battle. Another and often accepted story is that he was led before Edward IV, who, after some discussion with him, struck or pushed him. Thereupon the nobles gathered round Edward IV slew the young prince with their poniards. If the latter happened, it is a terrible commentary on the state to which English gentlemen had fallen after some years of civil war. Contrast it with the behaviour of the Black Prince to the captured King of France, one of his own class.

Young Edward died bravely as befitted the heir of Henry V, and the descendant of a line of kings. He was avenged on the king who slew, or allowed his slaying, in a terrible manner.

Edward IV was now securely settled on the throne. The poor old Henry VI was removed, by murder it seems, and Margaret kept in prison for five years until she was released to become the pensionary of Louis XI of France.

As for the young widow of Edward, the Lady Anne, she was, in 1473, only some eighteen months after the death of her husband, married to the Duke of Gloucester, one of those who was said to have murdered Edward.

The terrible tragedy of the Plantagenets was not yet finished. Edward IV had two sons. Of these, the elder, Edward of York, or of the Sanctuary, was made Prince of Wales at the age of six in 1477. He was called of the Sanctuary because he had been born in the Sanctuary at Westminster Abbey, where his mother, the former Elizabeth Woodville, had repaired when her husband, Edward IV, had had to flee from England.

So the young prince was born in the Sanctuary and there remained until his father had beaten all his enemies and come to lead queen and prince from the Abbey to the Tower.

The king took the greatest interest in the education of his son and was most anxious that he should not follow in the paths which he was treading so lustily. Edward IV was a bold wencher and loved the citizens and their wives, and daughters. His name is always linked with that of Jane Shore, but, in fact, his invasions of lovely womankind were

not confined to Shore or his queen. Still, he wished his son
to be innocent and his wish was granted.

The story goes that the king began to be much interested in
horoscopes and that he was skilled sufficiently to cast his son's.
He was horrified to find that no son of his should reign after
him, but that the throne would pass to his eldest daughter, the
Princess Elizabeth. This is probably a legend created after
the event, but the story could be true.

To use Winston Churchill's phrase, at the age of only
forty-two this strong king knew that his account was closed.
He had ruled England wisely and, despite his warlike upbringing, had devoted himself to peaceful pursuits. He had
encouraged commerce, and declined war with France, while
wisely keeping the money voted by Parliament for the purpose,
and at the same time accepting a large sum from Louis XI to
leave French soil.

When Edward lay dying he may have thought of the means
by which he reached the throne, and of his murder or permitted
murder of hapless Edward of Westminster after Tewkesbury.
He may have thought the more of this as he thought of his
own son, Edward V. For none knew better than Edward IV
the duplicity and cruelty of his brother, Richard of Gloucester.

Strange indeed were the fates in the matter of the overthrow
of the Plantagenets. The Lady Anne, married to her first
husband's slayer, was to reach the throne she had been promised
by Edward, Prince of Wales. She was to become queen through
her second husband's removal of the young Edward V, and her
own son was to be proclaimed Prince of Wales, but not to live
to see his father's overthrow.

The education of the Prince of Wales who became Edward
V was not only matter of concern to the king, his father, but
also, allowing for the centuries between, bore remarkable
resemblance to the hard and stern curriculum laid down for
the benefit of that Edward, Prince of Wales, who was to be
Edward VII. Take away the masses, which Edward IV as a
matter of course expected his young, almost infant son, to
attend, and put in their place longer hours of scholastic education and we can say that despite the four hundred years
between Edward V and Edward VII there is great similarity

in the upbringing. Each young prince was to have his youthful life made hard for him.

The training given to Henry V produced a great king, and it was the training which in the older time it was thought meet to give a Prince of Wales. But from the more literary period of the fifteenth century, when the countries of western Europe were waking from the sleep of the Middle Ages, education began to be more and more correlated with clerical work. It is not surprising to hear that King George V "held that it was no part of the duties of his elder sons to have access to such confidential information"; that is, that concerning international and commonwealth affairs. "Not even in the case of the Prince of Wales did the king permit his presence at audiences granted to Ministers" (Mr. John Wheeler Bennett, *Daily Telegraph*, 24th September 1958). Shades of Henry V, President of the Council at twenty years of age! This strange attitude to education of the heir to the throne came in at a later date than the reign of Edward IV, but the foundations of the change were laid then.

Like his predecessors, Edward V was from a tender age expected to have some interest in and knowledge of matters of state. He was sent down to Ludlow Castle when he was twelve in order to have a good influence on the Welsh people, who are said to have obeyed his commands very well.

The little prince did not have further opportunity to learn of statecraft except by the direst experience. He soon fell into the hands of his uncle, the famous or infamous Richard Crookback. Hardly had the boy been lovingly hailed by his subjects as Edward V than he disappeared into the Tower, never to be seen alive again outside its walls. By a skilful combination of cunning and ability in national affairs Richard, Duke of Gloucester made himself king in place of his nephew. Then little more was heard of the little Edward or his brother, Richard. No one knows what happened to them. The story with which everyone is familiar is that they were murdered at the command of Richard III. The little princes in the Tower have become figures of romance, like the babes in the wood. There are many people in English history alone of whom we are compelled to say that we do not know the fate. Arthur of Brittany, the inconvenient nephew of King John, vanished without trace, and so did the princes in the Tower. As so often happens when the black pigments of propaganda have been too liberally applied, there has been a reaction in favour of Richard III. He has been depicted in some works as though he were almost a white knight without fear or without reproach, dying nobly for his country, against the monstrous tyranny of Henry VII. In fact no one knows what happened, but reconstituted history is apt to require more credulity than the old version. To assume that Richard, having deposed his nephew, kept him and his brother in happy and honourable surroundings but so closely immured that no one outside the Tower knew where they were; to suppose, further, that on arrival in London Henry VII found the boys alive and well, and then proceeded to murder them, will be found in the end to demand a greater faith than the old simple story of a wicked uncle and two hapless babes.

Whatever the truth, and it is unlikely ever to be known, Richard III lost no time in making his own son, Edward of Middleham, Prince of Wales. No clearer indication could be given that Richard had no intention of playing any regent's part in the kingdom. He meant to perpetuate the dynasty of York in his own line. Edward of Middleham was Richard's son by Anne, widow of the Lancastrian Prince of Wales, murdered or otherwise slain, after Tewkesbury. He was ten years old when his father assumed the Crown. Very little is known about this boy, not unnaturally considering that for nine years of his life he lived at Middleham in Yorkshire, where he was born in 1474. During those years Richard, his father, the Duke of Gloucester, governed the north of England. He recovered from the Scots the considerable gains which they had made during the reign of poor Henry VI. Richard, who was a devout man, founded in Yorkshire several monasteries and endowed others.

When the duke became the king he gave the most earnest care to the young prince. He invested the boy twice with garland, ring and sovereign rod. He described the boy as one so well endowed that "by the favour of God he will make an honest man". Edward was Richard's only legitimate son, and it must have been a terrible blow to the king when the boy died. This happened in April 1484 when Richard was almost at the end of his first popularity with the masses of the people and when the growlings of rebellion were beginning to be detected from across the sea. Queen Anne, who had known so much sorrow, was dying, and in the following March, 1485, her body was buried in Westminster Abbey. It was in August that Richard III died fighting against the invading Earl of Richmond, afterwards Henry VII.

At Bosworth Field in Leicestershire in 1485 the old dynasty of England went down before the new family of Tudor. It is usual to regard this battle as the last of the Wars of the Roses, and to say that it marks the close of the Middle Ages in England. This is not a bad idea, for a good central date is useful as an aide-mémoire, but it must not be pressed too strongly. It is often said that the English nobility destroyed themselves in the Wars of the Roses and that only three noble houses survived that struggle. I have shown elsewhere how incorrect this is. (See footnote at end of chapter.) In fact what happened was that the nobles destroyed their own power. They showed themselves so selfishly indifferent to their country and her fortunes, whether abroad or at home, that in future they had no popular support. They ceased to be able to struggle with the sovereign. It seems curious at times that after a ding-dong battle during the whole of the Middle Ages, which wore out even the strongest kings, the monarchy should have triumphed just at the opening of the modern age. But it was just those modern forces which enabled Henry VII to render the nobles powerless.

For a few years of Henry's reign his throne was not entirely secure, but once the plots and rebellions engendered by thirty years of civil strife had been destroyed Henry VII was a stronger king than England had known since the days of William the Conqueror.

Before going on to deal with this situation and its reflection in the training of the Princes of Wales, there is a fascinating parallel between the closing scenes of the Plantagenet dynasty and the scenes in which it entered England. Richard III was the direct descendant of William the Conqueror (he was the great-great-great-great-great-great-great-great-great-great-grandson of William), though his line came through the Conqueror's granddaughter, Matilda, whose son was Henry II, of Anjou, who was the first of the Plantagenets. William obtained the kingdom of England by force and fraud. He admitted on his deathbed that he had no right to the English throne but had obtained it by wrong. The properly elected English king (election still remains as a relic in the English coronation service) was Harold; he was slain and his army defeated at the battle of Hastings, one of the most momentous battles of the world's history. William reigned in his stead, and his rights, at which a purist may not care to look, were soundly bolstered up by violence. Then for four hundred years, from 1066 to 1485, William's descendants reigned. It would be unfair and absurd to suggest that during the whole of that long period England did not know periods of greatness; but almost throughout the whole time she was bedevilled by the connection with France which began through William's conquest. Before the Norman Conquest England had no traditional hostility to France, and the two countries, in so far as they had any relations at all, were friendly. Intermarriage with princesses took place, and visits were exchanged. There was no inherent reason for the enmity of English and French to develop. Then came a king of England whose first interest was across the Channel. All his successors were the same. War succeeded war, and the Hundred Years War, in which England was the aggressor and in which she suffered less than France, was only the worst part of a long and bitter debate with the French.

With the battle of Bosworth the Plantagenets came to an end. Henry VII married the Princess Elizabeth, the daughter of Edward IV. He was careful to murder (by legal process) the last male of the Plantagenets, Edward, Earl of Warwick. Henry VIII waited another forty years before he removed the last of the Plantagenets, Margaret, Countess of Salisbury. Through Queen Elizabeth (wife of Henry VII) the Tudors were able to claim Plantagenet blood, and so through them the Stuarts and the Hanoverians, but it was a Plantagenet blood which was attenuated and despised or hated, for Henry

VII married Elizabeth of York only because she was needful to him for his throne.

The days of Plantagenet greatness were over, and they had ended as they had begun. Just as the great progenitor, William, had won a throne by force, so the last of his descendants to reign lost his throne on the field of battle. The body of Harold was treated with more consideration than that of Richard III, whose corpse was flung over a pack-horse and carried thus to Leicester with a halter round its neck. As no one knows now where Harold's ashes lie or where his bones found their last resting-place,[1] so none knows what happened to Richard's body, for, though interred at Leicester, it remained there only some fifty years. In the general fate of the monasteries, the bones were scattered.

In the strife of the Wars of the Roses 100,000 men, it has been estimated, perished, and for the sole ultimate end of destroying the colourful nobility of the country and rendering the monarchy supreme.[2] The only counterpoise to the throne was the Church, and this pillar of state was soon to be shaken. The new dynasty was to make laws to prevent the retention of armed bands by the nobles. In every age since 1485 the English aristocracy has been augmented by the rising men of the time. The sovereign wished to create a noble, and he did in fact ennoble his blood, and from this period dates the rise of a nobility with titles and wealth but without armed power.

In all this the question of the upbringing of the Prince of Wales was greatly affected.

[1] Tradition has placed Harold's burial place at Waltham Abbey, but there is no tomb there now.

[2] In my book, *The Story of the Peerage* (Blackwoods), I have included an appendix giving particulars of eighty-eight peerages created between 1392 and 1466. It is clear that many nobles' houses did survive the battles and the scaffolds of the Roses' war. Of course there were many cases in which the nobles perished in battle or soon after. In 1445, at the first battle of St. Albans, the Duke of Somerset, the Earl of Northumberland, and Lord Clifford fell among the Lancastrians. The Yorkist Lord Clinton died. After the battle of Wakefield it became the general custom to kill any lords who had been captured. They were usually executed without trial. This savagery had its effect. The people of England grew so weary of the fighting that they looked with satisfaction to a king who would keep order and prevent nobles from doing as they liked. But there were plenty of nobles left in the England which emerged from the Wars of the Roses.

CHAPTER VII

The Brother Princes—the Tudors

THE new dynasty of the Tudors made a clean sweep of many things which had been features of the medieval England. For one thing Henry VII's claim to the Crown was so poor that he had to be audacious and resolute in his handling of matters or he would have been condemned out of existence. He was the direct descendant of Edward III but through an illegitimate line. John of Gaunt, the fourth son of Edward III, had married, as his third wife, his former mistress, Katherine Swynford. His children by Swynford were legitimised, and John Beaufort, Duke of Somerset, was the great-grandfather of Henry VII. Then, in the male line, Henry's ancestors had the usual traditional descent of Welsh families—at least Henry said that they did. In fact, soon after ascending the throne Henry sent commissioners into Wales to look for his forebears, of note and fame. The results of the commissioners' findings have never been prominently displayed.

Henry's best claim to the throne lay in the weariness of the English people with the perpetual disturbances caused by the great lords; in addition to which the king had prudently married the Princess Elizabeth, the heiress of York. Thus came about the Tudor Rose, which is a product of art, not of horticulture. The Tudor Rose symbolised the end of the strife of the rival roses.

There was one aspect of the Tudor ascent to the throne which had great value among the Welsh and with reference to the Princes of Wales. This was the old prophecy of Cadwallader, the last King of the Britons, that his people would once more possess the land of their ancestors. When the last of the great

Norman-Angevin line had been killed at Bosworth, Lord Stanley took the Crown from the bush where it had fallen and placed it on the head of the Earl of Richmond, Henry Tudor. For the first time since 1066 Wales had a king of native origin and blood.

A Welshman had become King of England. He hastened to give to his son a name which would ring through Wales, and be of great moment in England also. This was the name of Arthur. Sir Thomas Kendrick has shown how much this name of the hero king of the popular mythology meant in the England and Wales of the Tudor period. The popular idea of the history of Britain was derived from the history of Geoffrey of Monmouth. Most modern writers disbelieve in Geoffrey of Monmouth's statement that he had derived his information from an old book brought over by a friend of his from Brittany. However, the truth of Geoffrey's history apart, there is no doubt of the great influence which it exercised on the thoughts of the Middle Ages in England. The *Historia Regum Britanniae*, or *British History* or *The Brut*, written by Geoffrey of Monmouth, described how Brutus the Trojan came from Troy about 1170 B.C. and conquered Britain. From him descended a long line of British or English kings, including Arthur, the hero of the Arthurian legends, right down to Cadwallader, who had been defeated by the Saxons.

The fortunes of this history, which at first carried all before it, and which is now discredited, do not matter so much in the present work, except to point out that the name of Arthur had a peculiar significance and that its use for the name of Henry VII's eldest son was deliberate. The boy was born in 1486, and from the start great things were expected of him. He was to revive the fame of his great namesake, and at many a pageant Arthur was hailed as the new Arthur come again to raise England and make it the terror of Europe. Arthur was supposed to have conquered most of Europe in his day and although none of this was known to historians outside the British Isles, that meant little to patriotic Englishmen.

Thus the legend of the British history gave the name of Arthur a lustre which aided the popularity of Henry VII. Even after Arthur had died at an early age, the reflection of the

Arthurian story still continued to attract the minds of English people. Francis Bacon, writing his history of Henry VII a century after Arthur's death, noted that the king, Henry VII, "in honour of the British race, of which himself was, named Arthur, according to the name of that ancient worthy king of the Britons, in whose acts there is truth enough to make him famous, besides that which is fabulous". In Edmund Spenser's *Faerie Queen*, written past the middle of the reign of Elizabeth I, the story of *The Brut*, and of Brutus come from Troy, is assumed throughout.

This young prince, then, who was born in September 1486 at Winchester, was destined by his father to be the glorious successor to himself. Winchester, his birthplace, added to his fame and the ambitious hopes held out for him, for was not Winchester closely associated with King Arthur, and was the Round Table not at Winchester?

The Prince Arthur was identified, then, with King Arthur and written down as the inheritor of his glories. Yet there was another Arthur in British history whose name might have been remembered as a bad omen. He was the Plantagenet prince whose death has never been satisfactorily explained. Arthur of Brittany had been the son of King John's elder brother Geoffrey. He should have been king in place of John.

Arthur of Winchester was christened with immense splendour at Winchester, only four days after his birth, this nearness of baptism to the birth day being the custom of those times. A great concourse of nobles was present at the ceremony, and everything was done to suggest the greatness of the infant.

Two other sons were born to Henry VII and Queen Elizabeth. Of these, Edmund lived only from February 1498 to January 1499. He was the youngest son of the king. The second son was a strong and vigorous child, named Henry, who was born in 1491. He was created Duke of York, but was not considered as of much account while his elder brother Arthur lived.

There were four daughters, of whom Elizabeth and Katharine died young. The two other girls were Margaret and Mary. Margaret married the King of Scots, James IV, and is the ancestor of all the sovereigns of England since 1603. Mary married Louis XII of France and, when he died, Charles Brandon, Duke of Suffolk. She was the grandmother of the tragic Lady Jane Grey.

The king's hopes centred upon Prince Arthur. He was created Prince of Wales when not four years old. His education proceeded with a grim rigour which allowed no chance for the boy to build up a strong constitution. From the earliest years Arthur was put on to learning, and under the skilled direction of his tutor, Bernard Andreas, he made remarkable strides. He learned to read Latin and Greek authors (whether the latter were in the original or in a Latin translation is not clear). Certainly the young prince was a good Latinist. He has left letters written to his future bride which are models of Latin style. Just at that time the air of England began to be disturbed, then invigorated and purged, by the classical revival. Greek began to be taught, and with the study of Greek and Latin authors a new horizon—a Renascence or New Birth period—opened out before men.

The strain of so much learning was lightened for the prince by his sport of archery. So good was he as an archer that he gave his name to outstanding proficients in the art; they were said to be true Prince Arthurs.

From the earliest age the young prince was the unconscious subject of matrimonial intrigues. There were several foreign princes who were willing to ally themselves with the House of Tudor. When negotiations were in progress between Spain and England on the subject of Prince Arthur's marriage the business nearly broke down owing to the demands of Henry VII. That king had known a great deal of poverty in his youth, and loved to feel that he had money in his coffers. His love of money was to lead in the sequel to a terrible amount of suffering.

The object of the king's choice for his son was the daughter of the King and Queen of Spain. This was Katharine of Aragon, the daughter of Ferdinand of Aragon and Isabella of Castile. Under these two who had been politically married, all Spain had become united and was about to enter upon her great career of conquest. The approach to Henry came from the Spanish king, and the ambassadors were permitted to view the young prince with nothing on (he was only a year old at the time) in order the better to appreciate his beauty and the value he would have for their young princess, Katharine, then only three years old.

When Henry VII wanted more dowry money than the Spanish ambassadors seemed able to give, they hinted to the king that his title was none too good, and that in view of what happened to the English kings he should be happy to make a match for his son with the sovereign of Spain, a great and settled land.

However, Henry VII was a man of persevering character and he gradually wrought upon the Spanish envoys, so that they returned home with lyrical accounts of the young Prince Arthur.

In due course the Princess Katharine of Aragon arrived in England to be married to young Arthur, to whom she had, indeed, been married more than once by proxy. To make the match possible, Henry VII had executed the last male heir of the Plantagenets, Edward Earl of Warwick, who died at the age of twenty-four for no other crime save that he was the male heir of the Plantagenets. He was put to death solely for that reason—because he threatened the king's throne, and his death was promised to the Spanish envoys, to show that no rival claimant to the English throne existed.

When the Prince Arthur first met his bride, he was shy and downcast, and little wonder. He was fifteen when he married her in November 1501; he had been wooing her for seven years, and writing letters to her in choice Latin. She, poor creature, was only two years older than Arthur, and when she said goodbye to her native land she had no idea that she would never see it again, and that she would long for the protection of its people. Her life in her English home was marked by many vicissitudes, and she must often have longed to return to sunny Spain and to the carefree days of her youth.

There was a good deal of bashfulness in Arthur's demeanour towards his bride, as well there might be. There had been between the young prince and princess four proxy weddings, beginning with one when the prince was in his cradle. When he did at last meet his bride he could speak to her only through

Henry Stuart, Prince of Wales, 1610: died before his father, James I.

George Augustus, son of George I, Prince of Wales, 1714: afterwards
George II.

the intermediation of a bishop who understood Spanish. Arthur had written his love letters in Latin.

The arrangement of the marriage of a prince and princess of those days is instructive, at least. The whole matter was in the hands of the parents, particularly the fathers of the two parties. Henry VII was a close-fisted Welshman who never forgot his early parsimonious upbringing. Ferdinand of Spain was equally averse to parting with money. Among the Spanish king's chief economies had been the paring down of the funds for Columbus's voyage across the Atlantic. It was not the fault of Ferdinand that the expedition had not failed. Indeed, it was only the sacrifices of Queen Isabella, who pawned her own jewels, which made Columbus's voyage possible. It can therefore easily be imagined what a match these two kings must have been for each other. It was some considerable time before the Spaniards could be brought to entrust their princess to the seas on her voyage to England, and her dowry had been a matter of haggling for years before it was partially settled. Once the Princess Katharine was in England her money was promptly seized by Henry VII, who undertook to look after it for the young couple. On his part Henry had had to carry out several very unpleasant actions for the sake of effecting the marriage. The death of the last male Plantagenet, the young Earl of Warwick, had been necessitated by the fact that the Spanish ambassador had pointed out the uncertainty of Henry's tenure of the throne. Henry VII had not hesitated long before clearing from his path the awkward impediment of the young earl's life. A few trumped-up charges, a mock trial and it was all over. More difficult was the charge that the Tudors were an upstart dynasty. This charge was unfortunately true, but as events were to prove the Tudors were also to be more beneficial to their country than all the other lines of royalty which had reigned over it.

Henry VII's policy was to establish his dynasty by marrying off his children to neighbouring sovereigns. He was very successful, for while Arthur (and afterwards Henry VIII) married into the Spanish dynasty, Henry VII's daughters married into the royal lines of France and Scotland. In none of these cases did the wishes of the children have any effect upon the ideas which Henry VII had conceived. Margaret was forced to marry James IV of Scotland, though both bride and groom were unwilling. Mary became for a short while the old man's darling of the King of France, and it was only her own strong Tudor will which eventually enabled her to marry the Duke of Suffolk. So all was fixed by the politic father in England, and he brought the bright Spanish girl to his elder son. Bright she seems to have been, for she enjoyed singing and dancing, and when she met her bridegroom she danced for his benefit with some of her ladies. Now that the years of arguing between the two greedy fathers were over, all was magnificence and gaiety in England. There were costly jousts and celebrations, public displays and grand preparations for the wedding. Eventually, on 14th November 1501, Arthur and Katharine were married at St. Paul's Cathedral; even then, when Henry (afterwards Henry VIII) was only eleven years old, it was he and not Arthur who led forth the bride not only before the wedding but afterwards when the party returned to the Bishop of London's Palace. There was something odd about this; it was as if the young Duke of York were destined to be the princess's husband.

Much disputation was to take place later on about this marriage, and even as to whether it had been consummated. After the wedding day came the wedding night, and Arthur, aged fifteen, and his bride, aged eighteen, were brought to bed. The morning after, the story went, his chamberlain came to him, as was his custom, and was surprised when he asked for a drink. On the chamberlain remarking that this was not his usual custom, Arthur answered that he had been in Spain where it was hot, and that to have a wife was a fine pastime. Yet there were those who said that a grave matron lay between the young couple on their first night.

It seems curious that there should have been arguments or disputes about such intimate matters. After two weeks the Prince and Princess of Wales went down to Ludlow, the royal seat on the Welsh marches, where the Princes of Wales were wont to exercise their authority over their Welsh liegemen. Here they stayed for some four and a half months, and here Arthur died suddenly on 2nd April 1502.

The blow to the king and queen was very great. The king seems to have put all his hopes on his elder son, while he gave to his younger son, Henry, an excellent education to fit him, possibly, for a clerical career; the shock of the sudden death was all the greater. The poor queen, whose life had not been very happy, came to console the king; he in his turn had to console her. Among the queen's comforts was her remark that she and the king were still capable of having children. Soon after the queen lost her life in trying to bear another child, who turned out to be a daughter.

The king, Henry VII, genuinely mourned for his elder son, although he did not ordinarily show any human feeling. Some years earlier he had drawn up some rules for the burial of a prince of royal blood, and now these rules were available for the burial of his child and first-born.

The young prince was buried in Worcester Cathedral, and the obsequies were almost as impressive as the celebrations of the wedding had been. All the officers of the prince's household had their several duties to perform, and broke their staves and cast them into the grave, while the heralds who gave out the titles of the deceased high and mighty prince took off their tabards and cast them into the grave likewise. The Earl of Kildare rode the young prince's horse into the cathedral and offered the dead youth's arms and armour.

Once the prince had been buried the predominant thought in the mind of the king was the dowry which his daughter-in-law had brought with her. This amounted to 200,000 crowns, half of which had been paid over. The idea of this sum being sent back to Spain proved too much for the king. He soon, as already mentioned, became a widower, and the first thought which came to him was that he should marry Katharine himself. No-one in that age would have thought anything wrong in such an idea. Policy ruled everything then, and for a man of fifty to espouse a girl of eighteen would have seemed quite right if the marriage served some purpose of state. However, Ferdinand of Spain tried to dissuade Henry, and suggested another of his daughters, Juanna of Castile. This daughter was mad, but the wise Ferdinand did not think that Henry need worry over this as mental incapacity would not prevent her from bearing children, which was the main reason why she was wanted. Juanna's particular hallucination consisted in the belief that her husband was not dead, hence her refusal to have his body buried.

Meanwhile Katharine lived a most wretched life. She had been granted a third of the revenues of Wales, Chester and Cornwall, but these were never paid to her, while her dowry had been seized by Henry VII. Arthur died in 1502, and it was not until 1509, after Henry VIII had ascended the throne, that Katharine was married to him. During those eight years Katharine lived in extreme poverty and at times was dunned by creditors. Before she had reached the age of thirty she was thoroughly experienced in poverty and adversity. Her father would not help her; his advice to her was that she should catch the new Prince of Wales, Henry; her father-in-law refused to be responsible for her debts or to allow her sustenance. Her letters were opened and read and she had no means of communication except through channels watched by others.

The real cause of all the trouble was her money. Henry VII was only concerned with that, and he was quite willing to overlook everything else provided that he could have Katharine's dowry. He agreed to the marriage with Arthur's brother, Henry. One obstacle had to be cleared out of the way, and that was the ecclesiastical commandment that a man should not take his brother's wife. The only thing to do was to have recourse to the Pope. It was considered that even in the event that the marriage between Arthur and Katharine was a valid union—and, as mentioned, there were doubts as to whether it had ever been consummated—the removal of difficulties lay within the papal power. It was held that the Pope could remove any obstacles to the marriage with a deceased brother's widow. So petitions were made to Pope Julius II for the permission of the Church that Henry and Katharine should marry. The upshot of the negotiations with the Pope was that Julius II had granted a full dispensation for the marriage to take place, and had provided for every contingency which could be thought of, so that even if the marriage of Arthur and Katharine were a fully consummated marriage, the marriage of Henry and Katharine could still proceed.

Prince Henry, for his part, was eager for the marriage. The mature beauty of Katharine made its appeal to him, perhaps from the first moment when he met her, and he willingly agreed to marry her when the papal dispensation should have been obtained.

Henry had the utmost respect for the Pope and the teachings of the Church. His education had been almost as bookish as that of his brother.

The young princes were educated not only by Bernard Andreas, already mentioned, but by the famous Linacre, who had studied Greek, natural sciences and medicine. Skelton, the poet, was also a teacher of Henry.

The accounts which we have of the education of the young nobility in the period of the Renaissance make one wonder not that many youths died, worn out with the struggle to absorb too much knowledge, but rather that any survived.

Arthur had at an early age read authors as various as Homer, Virgil, Lucan, Ovid, Plautus, Terence, Cicero, Quintillian, Thucydides, Livy, Caesar, Suetonius, Tacitus, Pliny, Sallust and Eusebius. This is a fairly extensive list covering a vast range of the ancient classical writers. When we think that, in addition to reading the above, Arthur would also have the observances of religion on a much more exacting scale than at present, even in a royal family, and that he was expected, and indeed required, to have some useful pastimes such as archery, dancing, and the chase, it would seem that pressure upon the nerves and constitution is nothing new. The marvel is that Arthur stood up to this type of training for so long. His brain must have been tired beyond expression, and his body exhausted by the strain of work.

Henry, his brother, was made of sterner stuff. His early training was hard, and he combined the hard mental labour involved in all education in those days with a great range of physical accomplishments. He read St. Thomas Aquinas and practised tilting. He loved to hunt and to wear his armour. He became a good musician, leaving behind him pieces of music of rare delight and mostly of a religious style. He had many suits of rich armour designed for him, and he was a gallant jouster in the lists. He loved religious services and often attended five masses in a day. He loved study and theological debate. There is something in the story that Henry VII had destined his younger son to the archiepiscopal see of Canterbury. Who knows what ambitious projects the father had nursed while his other children were allied with the royal houses of Europe? Perhaps he had hope of the papal chair for his younger son.

Thus the education of a Prince of Wales in the fifteenth–sixteenth centuries showed no decline in quality from that of an earlier period. In fact it was becoming harder; and although some forms of princely education had become obsolete, others had arrived to take their place in the regal catalogue and curriculum. The education of the two Tudor princes shows the influence of the Renaissance, and the combination of study with the pastime which makes a full man: a firm mind in a firm body. Henry measured up to this, but Prince Arthur could not.

When Henry VIII came to the throne, with the full applause of his subjects, he was one of the most admired princes in the world. He was young and handsome, with a fine skin, which showed when he was playing tennis. He glowed with health and energy. He loved life in all its forms and was made for a happy home life. He had bent to his father's will, and had been prepared for the priesthood, but could not have felt anything but joy when he knew that a life in the world was the life for him. To the end of his days he was to be interested intensely in theological discussions, and to take a personal interest in the doctrinal struggle caused by Protestantism. Had he been ordained a priest it is possible that his life would have resembled that of a Renaissance Pope, rather similar to that of Wolsey, who was the father of two children and a pluralist holder of livings who had very little interest in the affairs of his dioceses.

However, Henry was redeemed for worldly uses and he came to the consideration of the world with zest. There were protracted negotiations between the courts of England and Spain. Into these he did not enter but they were to affect his future and that of his country, not to say of the world.

In the first place, the matter which had to be settled was

whom should the Princess of Spain, Katharine, marry? After her father had persuaded Henry VII to look in another direction, the matter did not remain as a serious political issue. Katharine of Aragon, if she married in England, had to marry Henry. That she had to look for her fortune in England was made abundantly clear to her by her father, who told her that there was nothing which he could do for her. It was Henry or penury in the English streets for Katharine. The conduct of both father and father-in-law was without excuse. Neither of them would do anything to help her.

There were powerful agencies at work labouring to bring about the marriage of Henry and Katharine. Of these the most powerful was that of money. The king, Henry VII, could not bear to lose Katharine's dowry. At all costs this must be retained in England. To do this it was necessary to get the papal consent to the marriage of Henry with his deceased brother's wife. "The main question involved was a simple one, Katharine had been married to Prince Arthur for the last four months of his sickly life. If that union had not been consummated, it was only a betrothal in the eyes of the law, and not a marriage, and there was no ground whatever for impugning the validity of the subsequent marriage between Henry and Katharine" (Wakeman's *History of the Church of England*, page 199). This quotation is made, of course, from a discussion of the divorce problems of Henry VIII, but it was the events of twenty years earlier which had such consequences.

The Pope Julius II did grant a dispensation by papal bull allowing the marriage of Henry and Katharine. He added some time later a brief which confirmed the bull of dispensation and guarded it against any possible objections. All this was done in order to meet the scruples of Henry VII, who feared that something might happen to prevent his keeping the dowry. The points were that, as stated in the above quotation, an unconsummated marriage was not a real marriage, and therefore as the marriage of Arthur in that event had been a nullity there was no bar against the subsequent marriage of Katharine to Henry. In addition, it must be understood that should the marriage of Arthur and Katharine have been real and valid, yet the dispensing powers of the Pope were considered equal to dispensing with the objection and with granting Henry permission to marry Katharine.

This was precisely what happened, and so the wedding bells rang for the poor Spanish princess who had already suffered so sorely in the England of her adoption. This was not, however, until after the death of Henry VII in 1509. Thirteen days before the coronation the new king, Henry VIII, married Katharine. This was in June 1509, and at the beginning of the New Year, 1510, a son was born, named Henry, Duke of Cornwall. Unfortunately he lived only a few weeks; there had been many cases of young princes dying before they had passed from the cradle, but in this case it was to prove more serious for the nation than most. For the moment the matter was overlooked because of the king's youth and his absorption in matters of foreign warfare. However, over a period of ten or twelve years he and his queen lived happily enough, but gradually the prospects of a male heir dwindled away. Children were born to Katharine but, with one exception, they did not live for long. The exception was the Princess Mary, born in 1515. She was to become, after a wretched earlier life, the unhappy queen who has gone down in history as Bloody Mary.

It is not so difficult to understand the impatience and the genuine forebodings of Henry VIII. True, after his early years with Queen Katharine he began to indulge himself and to take mistresses. One of these, Elizabeth Blount, bore him a son, whom he created Duke of Richmond. For this boy Henry VIII had such great love that he is said to have meditated on making him, though illegitimate, king after himself.

However, the king began to question within himself whether he had done right in marrying his brother's wife. Had the papal dispensation really made all clear? Did not Scripture forbid such a marriage in the strongest terms? Why did no male child live to inherit his throne? Behind these questions loomed the horrible thought of another disputed succession to the English throne.

Henry therefore applied to the Pope, Clement VII in this case, to set aside his predecessor's, Julius II's, bull and brief. We have seen how carefully these documents had been drawn. So Henry's request was tantamount to asking one Pope to undo

completely the most solemn act of another. The term divorce
in connection with the suggested dissolution of Henry's marriage
is liable to be misunderstood. There was no divorce under
church law then, any more than there is under the Roman
Catholic canon law now. Divorce was a term used in the
sense of nullifying a marriage. The casuists had worked very
hard and had produced a series of tests which enabled them
to overcome various obstacles and to nullify any marriage
unless fortified by the most determined means.

The task set before the Roman Curia was hard enough, but
it was complicated by the fact that the Pope was in the power
of the nephew of Katharine, the emperor Charles V, a mighty
sovereign. Clement may have felt that something should be
done to clear the question in Henry's interests, but he feared
very greatly the power of the master of Italy. If he gave a
decision against Katharine he would lose his liberty. Charles
V, however good a Catholic in his professions and practice,
had no hesitation in letting his troops storm Rome, as it had
not been stormed since the days of Alaric. In 1527 the troops
under the command of the Constable de Bourbon took Rome.
The Pope was a prisoner. This was the end of any hope of a
divorce, or rather nullity, in the case of Henry's marriage.
What would have happened had the Pope continued a free
agent? It seems likely that political considerations would have
made him give Henry what he wanted.

No political considerations were now to operate on Henry's
side. All was against him. The Pope received an appeal from
Katharine, and brought this into his own court at Rome.

Thus the aim of Henry's adviser, Cardinal Wolsey, had
failed. Instead of a divorce being successfully piloted through
the Roman Courts, the king found himself in the position
that he was unlikely to secure any relief at all from the Pope.
Meantime he had fallen in love with Anne Boleyn, the sister
of one of his former mistresses. She would not become his
mistress, but held out for marriage. The king now had all
the incentive of tempestuous passion to force him along the
path of a quarrel with Rome.

The king set himself to be free of the dragging chain of
Rome. He soon invoked the assistance of the nation by an

appeal to its patriotism. The exactions of the Popes were not popular and there had been many bitter quarrels in the past over the exercise of papal authority. There smouldered in many English minds a longing to be free, not of the Papacy as a religious force but of the Papacy as a taxgatherer and interferer.

By a series of measures, Henry VIII swept away the papal power between 1529 and 1534 and made himself the master of his realm as no king had before him. He overawed the clergy and dragged from them an acknowledgment of his supremacy. Nowhere was it suggested that the Pope was not the head of the Church but only that he had no jurisdiction in England to exact money and to interfere in home affairs.

During the long struggle, Henry became acquainted with Thomas Cranmer, a church lawyer who bent his great mental powers and experience entirely to the king's will. He was made Archbishop of Canterbury and lost no time in pushing through the divorce, which was almost a work of superogation, since the king had already quietly married Anne Boleyn. Everyone in England of any consequence was required to agree to the new marriage, and those who objected, like Sir Thomas More, were executed if they dared to speak out.

Anne Boleyn had staked her all upon giving Henry a son. She failed. Their first-born child was a daughter, Elizabeth I, but unfortunately Henry's heart was set upon a male heir. Anne's other child, also a Henry, Duke of Cornwall, died, again like his namesake and half brother, when not even a few days old. His death sealed the fate of Anne Boleyn. She was soon supplanted by her rival, Jane Seymour, who at last presented her lord and master with the only legitimate son of his ever to enter his teens. Edward VI, as that son afterwards became, was never made Prince of Wales. He was ten years old when Henry VIII died, and the patent for his creation as Prince of Wales was made out but Henry fell ill and died before the documents could be signed.

Thus fell the idea of a Prince of Wales, and no other was to be created for a century. The very use of the title must have passed out of mind. Courtiers might write verses to Elizabeth inviting her thoughts to the days when a new little Prince of

Wales would play in the royal palaces and come to resemble his wonderful grandfather, but alas the great Elizabeth never married.

Under Henry VIII, the daughters who were to succeed him were sometimes referred to in an informal manner as Princess of Wales, depending upon which, Mary or Elizabeth, was in favour at the time. The title has never, however, been granted to a woman.

CHAPTER VIII

The Brother Princes—the Stuarts

AFTER the passage of one hundred and one years England again had a Prince of Wales, and this time a Scotch prince, Henry of Stirling. He was the elder son and the heir of James VI of Scotland and I of England. There had been an enormous change in England since the last Prince of Wales had ascended the throne as Henry VIII.

For the first consideration, England had changed her religion. From a Catholic country she had become so Protestant that the very name of Papist was a term of abuse. From time to time there were rumours of Catholic plots and risings to put a Catholic on the throne or to convert the country to Catholicism by force. Certainly fear of Catholic plots did exist among the English people, from the nobles to the poorest of the people. In the Gunpowder Plot (1605) such a conspiracy did, in fact, materialize and justified the fears of all those who held that the Papists were capable of anything. In fact, the number of Catholics was not considerable and they could not have over-turned the state unless they had been able to destroy all the leaders of the nation, as Guy Fawkes and his friends had intended.

The whole outlook of the people had changed in matters of religion. While the outward framework of a Catholic church had been maintained, more by the efforts of Tudor sovereigns than from any other cause, the spirit of the people tended more to the extremer forms of Protestantism. It was not until the English people had had a taste of what Puritan rule really meant that they turned back to the episcopal church as it had been established under Elizabeth I. From 1662 onwards the prevailing tendency in England was in favour of the Established

Church, and half of the population at least would always describe itself as Church of England.

The Bible had taken the place of priestly authority, and prayer direct to God existed without the intercession of the Mother of God and of the saints.

In the first place, then, the sovereign of the land would have to be a Protestant. The last Catholic sovereign, Mary I, had done nothing to induce the people to return to Catholicism. The fires of Smithfield have only recently lost their glow in English hearts.

Next in importance to the religious change was the complete alteration of the social life of the country. When a Tudor Prince of Wales existed, the great lords and their squabbles were still fresh in the minds of the mass of the people. When James VI came south the bickerings of great lords were important to a small circle, but, despite the vast wealth of the nobility, they could not rule the land as Warwick the King-Maker had done.

Wealthy and powerful in their influence and patronage, the nobles whom James VI found awaiting him had not armed retainers who could disturb the state. All that dangerous nonsense had been ended by the Tudors. Under Elizabeth I some of the greatest nobles of the land had tried their hand at rebellion, only to find themselves utterly ruined, and either driven into hopeless exile or sent to the block. The fate of so great a lord as the Duke of Norfolk might have been taken as proof positive that the days of king-making were over.

In place, however, of the great lords with bands of ruffling followers there was a numerous and wealthy class of gentlemen, owners of landed estates, well equipped with money, and of reasonable education. They were to exercise a predominant influence in the state under the Stuart kings. They did it through Parliament.

Under the Tudors England had been threatened by all sorts of dangers. She had therefore submitted to a personal rule, never seen before or since in England. The Tudor monarchs had ruled the country as though it were their farm. They had ordered Parliament to cease debates, if they felt inclined, and Parliament had ceased. But the Stuarts could not do this.

James I lectured his Parliament as Elizabeth I had never done, but he could not control it as she had been able to do. Yet even the Tudors would have found that Parliament could no longer be controlled, as it had been in the sixteenth century. Economic forces had made their way to the fore. The country was richer, better provided than it had ever been. Wealth came in from all quarters. The dissolution of the monasteries had brought huge areas of land and much wealth into the royal exchequer, whence it soon made its way to time-servers and courtiers.

The discovery of the New World opened up possibilities of wealth, and English minds soon turned to the wonders of the far west. The growth of European trade, despite the very long war between Spaniards and Dutch, had been very great, and Sir Thomas Gresham had made London one of the money centres of the world.

Altogether it was a richer, more materialistic England, yet a more freedom-loving one, which now faced the new line of kings from Scotland.

On their part, the new royal family was accustomed to a very different atmosphere around a court from that which prevailed in England. However freedom-loving the English might be, they were not inclined to murder, as were the Scots on the least provocation or lack of it. They wished to reverence their sovereigns, to pay court to them. They wished them to be splendid but did not wish to provide them with too much money.

To James I it seemed that he had come into the land of plenty. He had mastered his Scottish kingdom but at the cost of much suffering. He had always to be on the watch against his own people. His nobles were always ready to plot against him. They could not be trusted. Then, on top of the misery and hard conditions of the Scottish royal house, there was poverty. When the visiting notables from a foreign land had to be amused, the Scottish exchequer was hard put to it.

The effect on James was to make him feel that he need worry about money no more. He had come into a rich haven where peace and plenty reigned and where men were anxious to give valuable prizes into his hands. This sense of well-being was delusive. He was the first Scotsman to perceive the finest sight in the world, the high road leading into England, but, unlike so many of his countrymen who have followed in his steps, James did not realize that success in the south attended on work, hard work, alone.

After reaching England James I abandoned attempt at really serious work except in spasms. He gave himself over to self-indulgence on a disgusting scale.

Of the children of James I and his Queen Anne of Denmark only three reached maturity. They were Henry of Stirling, his younger brother Charles, afterwards King Charles I, and Elizabeth, who became Electress Palatine and Queen of Bohemia.

Henry of Stirling was a fine, vigorous youth, and seemed destined to a long and brilliant reign. He was much beloved. His brother Charles was a sickly infant, whose life was despaired of in his early years.

Henry was brought up in seclusion at Stirling. He was born in 1594, and was thus in his tenth year when his father succeeded to the English crown. His education followed the pattern of that of a typical Rennaissance prince: culture, the dead and the living languages, physical exercise, archery, tournaments, wearing of armour, music and the arts, and, above all, a most complete grounding in theology.

With a father such as James I, Prince Henry could not escape a rigorous upbringing. James himself was one of the most learned men in Europe. He loved to write learned treatises. From the age of four the lonely boy had been subjected to the rule of George Buchanan and Peter Young. "They gar me speik Latin ar I could speik Scottis." This was James's description of their regimen. At six he was described as a very toward prince of his age both in wit and person. At eight he was capable of translating from Latin into French into English. He was thus educated along the same lines as Edward VI, but must have been made of stronger stuff, for James survived.

James by the time he reached man's estate was so well read and instructed in a wide variety of learning that he could, in the opinion of one recent writer, have professed several subjects at university level. Certainly he was a theologian of no mean skill. He would argue with his archbishops and bishops in England to his heart's content and could usually beat his opponents in a game of dialectics.

A man so brought up would want his son trained in the same manner, and from an early age Henry of Stirling was wont to send his father a Latin letter on regular occasions. He had progressed enough in Latin by the time he was nine to read Phaedrus, Terence and Cicero. James also enjoyed giving good advice, and wrote to his son on the care with which princes should conduct themselves. They were like gods on earth, and were accountable to God alone. Here was the Divine Right of Kings with a vengeance.

Henry absorbed as much as he wished of his father's advice. He was a dutiful son and did as he was bid, but he obeyed in the letter and in the spirit took his own line. He was trained well in martial exercises by Richard Preston, and rode, sang and danced. He was a good son in the sense that he carried out his father's wishes, but he was distant with him and never allowed James to show him the sort of affection which he loved to bestow upon Steenie (his name for Buckingham).

Henry soon came to England with his mother and Princess Elizabeth. He was well received. Much is in a name for a prince, and Henry appealed to Englishmen and they began to hope for a reviver of England's fame on the battlefield, as Henry V had done at Agincourt. Poems and papers flowed in on the prince urging him to press on to glorious things. He was to lead Englishmen to victory on foreign fields.

Henry of Stirling was of a fine, handsome countenance and became at once extremely popular and one on whom the hopes of the nation were set. His father cut such a feeble figure, especially by comparison with his mighty predecessor, Elizabeth I, that his heir was bound to shine by contrast with himself.

Prince Henry was very different from his father or his younger brother, Charles. James I had written out for the boy's guidance many sententious and wise precepts in his Basilikon Doron, which was the expression of the doctrine of Divine Right of Kings. But the growing boy could not fail to see how very different from his precepts were the king's practices. What was the good of talking about the virtues due in a kingly character, such as sobriety, when Henry may well have witnessed, and certainly must have heard, of the disgraceful scenes which marked the entertainment given to the King of Denmark, Christian IV? In passing, it may be noted that on this occasion a masque called that of Solomon and Sheba was to be presented to the Majesties of England and Denmark. Practically everybody was drunk at this spectacle and one of the principal performers was sick over the Danish king.

Then again, James told his son that no one person should be employed to the prejudice of others and to the detriment of the state. On top of this, Henry saw favourites such as Robert Carr, who although quite unfit to take any part in government, were none the less preferred before others and to whom the king gave a disgraceful form of affection. Consequently Prince Henry took a line of his own. Soon after his arrival in England he had his own household and began to lead his own life. He became very interested in the Navy and, accompanied by Phineas Pett, the Master Shipwright at Woolwich, he visited the Fleet and at the early age of fourteen knew more about it than his father or the members of the Council. Henry had an admiration for a man whom his father kept in prison—the great Sir Walter Raleigh. The famous remark "Only my father would keep such a bird in such a cage" was made openly by the prince. Outwardly dutiful, the prince yet evinced by such sayings the very different view which he took of affairs from his father. When an arranged marriage was proposed for him with a Catholic princess the prince acquiesced, as was expected of the heir to the throne, but remarked that two religions should never lie together in his bed.

The prince was born in 1594, and came to England with his mother, Anne of Denmark, soon after James had reached the English throne. In 1610 he was created Prince of Wales. He brought with him into England fresh titles for the heir to the throne—namely, those of High Steward of Scotland, Duke of Rothesay, Earl of Carrick, Lord of the Isles and Baron of Renfrew. These form part of the Prince of Wales's title to this day, but the old title of Prince of Scotland is not used.

The ceremony of creating Henry Prince of Wales was the

more magnificent because no prince had been so created in living memory. He went along the Thames to Westminster, where the king waited for him in the House of Lords. The king and a great number of peers all gorgeously apparelled awaited him. Prince Henry, attended by some noblemen, entered, clad in a surcoat of purple velvet and bareheaded. Advancing towards the throne, the prince bowed thrice, and then knelt before his father, while the letters-patent were read by the Earl of Salisbury. The king then put the robes of Prince of Wales upon him, girded him with the sword, invested him with the rod and the ring, and put upon his head the cap and coronet. The new-made Prince of Wales was then conducted to the left hand of King James, James should then have kissed the prince but first insisted on having his hand kissed by the prince, after which the king gave his son a hearty embrace. There was a magnificent banquet afterwards and the prince's titles were proclaimed in English, French and Latin. Some twenty knights were dubbed in honour of the occasion, each required to take a ceremonial bath, hence their title of Knights of the Bath.

At the creation of the Prince of Wales, his younger brother, Charles, Duke of Albany, made his first state appearance. Charles in his earliest days had very poor health. He could not walk properly until he was four, and it was longer before he could speak without impediment. Charles was brought to England, where in 1606 he was made Duke of York. Although he was then only six years old his household was arranged for him and various persons appointed to undertake his education. It seems that in those days the preceptors often wrote for their charges the portentous Latin epistles which the children were supposed to produce. None the less, education was a serious matter and nothing was spared in the effort to make a finished princeling. So Charles in the air of England began to thrive. He was his mother's favourite, and after his brother's death it appeared that he was also his father's.

Meanwhile, the hopes of the nation were centred on Prince Henry. He was regarded as a good Englishman, although he was of course by birth a Scotsman. He was certainly in agreement with several of the national prejudices, for he hated Spain and wanted to renew the Elizabethan aggressions against her. He was a sound Protestant, in an age when the failure of the Gunpowder Plot had made persecution of Catholics seem like a patriotic duty. He was a keen navy man. He loved sport, hunting, the tournament, and archery. He loved tennis. He was well educated but not pedantic. He had a clear, logical mind, and knew exactly what he wanted. His household at St. James's was large, to the number of four hundred or five hundred persons. He formed a brilliant court around him, and although he was only sixteen when created Prince of Wales he was soon the centre of attraction to all those who hoped for better things from James's heir than from James, or who worshipped the rising sun.

There was enough of splendour in the prince's court to make James jealous and to cause him to complain that he was being ousted from affairs by his son. When Henry was seventeen years old he requested that he should be appointed to preside over the Council. This meant that he would be sharing the executive power of government with the king. We can understand some of the allusions to Henry as a reviver of the fame of his namesake, Henry of Monmouth. Just as Henry V, when Prince of Wales, had been the President of the Council and had excited Henry IV's jealousy, so the prince excited the hostility of James I. The request was refused, and it is hard to know what the consequences might have been had Henry lived. It was thought that the refusal was due to the hostility of Robert Carr, the king's favourite, and as Carr soon afterwards fell from favour the prince might have renewed his request later with more success.

In 1612, when the prince was not yet eighteen, the blow fell. He sickened and died. The breach that had existed between him and his parents was now apparent, for the king and queen visited their son once only and then went away to deal with their grief in private, each in a separate palace. During his illness the prince called upon his friend, David Murray, and on the sister he loved so greatly, Elizabeth. The physicians were powerless against the disease, and finally reluctantly admitted the use of a remedy which the queen obtained from Sir Walter Raleigh. All failed, and Henry died, cut off, to the great grief of the nation, and especially of the growing Puritan section.

James and Anne soon recovered from the shock. They had the excuse that the Elector Palatine, the Palsgrave Frederick, had come to England to seek the hand of the Princess Elizabeth. As soon as some decency permitted, the betrothal took place, and mourning was worn at it. The wedding had great consequences, for from it sprang the House of Hanover, which was to rule England a century later.

Great as was the popular mourning for Henry, it is possible that he would, had he become Henry IX, have been a far more dangerous man than his father or brother from the constitutional point of view. His very virtues and intellectual powers would have made him far more formidable as a ruler.

The situation had now occurred once more whereby the sovereign's elder son, the Prince of Wales had died, and his younger brother, hitherto not much thought of, had to take his place. In 1616 the Duke of York was advanced to the title of Prince of Wales. No great ceremonies marked his creation, as though the parents were afraid to provoke Providence by their actions. It was at Ludlow, the seat of the Council of Wales, that the splendid ceremonies took place.

James I had nine more years to live, and during this time his mind, when he could tear himself from hunting and drinking and other indulgences, was still taken up with the prospects which had filled it since he knew that he was to be king of England as well as of Scotland. He had hoped to be the peacemaker of Europe, in politics and in religion. The kings and princes of Europe were to listen to his great wisdom, and even the Pope would see the wisdom of letting James treat him as the first Bishop of Christendom, without any claim to supremacy. James's ideas were good ones, but they just did not appeal to the politicians of his age. He spent nine years and more in negotiating a marriage with the Infanta of Spain, which never came off. During the wooing of the Infanta James and his son were made to look very foolish. Charles and Buckingham travelled across Europe under the names of John and Thomas Smith. Buckingham had supplanted Robert Carr as the recipient of James's indecent familiarities. To send the heir to the throne on an incognito mission to Spain in the seventeenth century was to beg for trouble, and trouble was nearly forthcoming. It is a new slant on the character of Charles I that he was prepared to go in disguise on a foolhardy errand and to vault over a wall into a garden in order to see the lady of his dreams. Spanish etiquette prevented any real courtship and Spanish bigotry prevented any really serious effort to bring about the marriage with the son of a Protestant prince. After several months spent in Spain Charles and Buckingham returned home. The king had meanwhile been writing letters to them urging Baby Charles (James loved pet names for his son also) and Steenie to come back. James used to slobber over his favourites, yet be anxious for them to marry. Once they had been married he fussed over their ladies and took as much interest in the arrivals of their babies as if he had been a normal man. So when he found that his "dear Baby" and Steenie were home his joy was extravagant. He kissed and cuddled them for all he was worth.

The Prince of Wales was to find solace for his wounded feelings. Repulsed by Spain, he found consolation in France, and was soon married to the Princess Henrietta Maria, who remained a Catholic. James's queen, Anne of Denmark, became a Catholic without too much concealment, and James and Charles were looked on as likely converts, while it was the opinion of the Jesuits that there were enough Catholics in England to make a change back to the old religion a matter of practical planning and expectation.

In March 1625 the old king died and Charles succeeded to his throne. King of three kingdoms, he was to lose them all. Those who were interested in omens declared that it was ominous that at the Coronation the sermon should have been preached from the text: "Be thou faithful unto death and I will give thee a crown of life."

Apart from the works mentioned later in the bibliography, a useful book for the period of James I is *The Wisest Fool in Christendom*, by William McElwee, 1958, Faber and Faber.

The reign of James I was, in the proper sense of that misused term, a period of transition. The Tudor machinery, which depended very much on patronage, was beginning to wear

down when Elizabeth I died, but it was under James that the
real trouble began to show itself. The circumstances of the
struggle between King and Parliament were being formed
in the reign of James I. It is easy to be disgusted by the character
of James I, there is much which is unlovely in his make-up,
but it would have required a much abler monarch than he to
have brought his expenditure into line with his income. James
went on from financial crisis to crisis, and rejected all proposals
which could make him solvent. He could not govern without
a parliament, but when one had been called he could not
resist the opportunity to lecture his parliament men on their
duties. The growing independence of the age responded to
this pedagogy with irrelevant truisms, such as that the Scots
had not suffered above two of their kings in two hundred years
to die in their beds.

In the economic sphere the country was growing richer, and
it was also a period in which many distinguished men flourished.
The work of Shakespeare was to be at its best under James.
Harvey discovered the circulation of the blood; the Authorised
Version of the Bible was produced, one of the greatest miracles
of literature.

Abroad, the Continent was being divided into the two camps
which were to keep their distinct lines for nearly two hundred
years. The Catholic Counter-reformation had seemed at first
likely to recover the old heritage of the Church, but despite its
vast successes in southern Europe the Catholic revival was
spent. Not until the nineteenth century did Catholicism begin
to recover ground in the north and west of Europe.

In the course of this study I have commented on the changes
wrought by time in the mode of education of our Princes of
Wales. Nowhere is this change more clearly indicated than
in the rules for the household of Prince Henry. There was the
greatest care to ensure that ragged and unwholesome persons
were not allowed near his person. Nor were loose women
allowed around the royal apartments. They were to be driven
away.

The etiquette of the prince's court required that his servants
should at all times be decently clad whenever they approached

him. Their behaviour was to be decorous, and their clothes correctly done up, and not in disarray. The officials of the prince's household were to take Holy Communion four times a year, and were advised to take it twelve times.

Wages were set out in an orderly manner, and everything was regulated to the most minute detail. It is not remarkable that princes so reared should entertain ideas of greatness which sprang only from their rank.

One of the most notable features in the story of the Stuart princes is the love felt for Buckingham by both King James I and Charles, Prince of Wales. Buckingham was at first repulsive to Charles, but the cunning favourite did not need anything but an opportunity to woo the prince. Charles had never received much attention, till at the death of his brother he became the heir to the throne. Buckingham skilfully ingratiated himself with the prince.

Charles and Buckingham became fast friends, and it was only Buckingham's tragic death at Portsmouth that dissolved the alliance, and left Charles without a friend or adviser whom he liked.

We have next to deal with a century of further changes, and not least in the material connections of the title Prince of Wales.

CHAPTER IX

Fugitive Princes and Princes in Exile

WITH the accession of Charles I there begins in the story of the Princes of Wales a century in which battle, disaster, exile and proscription are the lot of the heirs to the throne.

At first it seemed, indeed, that the reign of Charles I would be a fortunate and happy period. Not that he began on friendly terms with his Parliament. Almost in his first year money troubles, and arguments as to how money should be raised, made the relations between King and Parliament sadly lacking in harmony. Charles had inherited more than his share of his father's obstinacy. His extremely bad health as a youth coupled with the fact that he had not really expected to take the place of his brilliant brother, had not helped him to prepare adequately for the throne. Then his friendship with Buckingham meant that he had as adviser and friend one who was undoubtedly brilliant but lacking in any serious understanding of the problems which confronted Charles. James I had been, in one way, fortunate in dying as a prematurely aged man of sixty. Had he lived much longer the terrible chaos in which his finances had fallen would have caused disastrous trouble in the state.

The truth was that the methods of the Tudors in governing the country had outlived their usefulness. Under James I many of the difficulties which Elizabeth I had overcome by sheer personality had been rendered acute. Any king coming to the throne in 1625 would have been in difficulties over the supply of money. Had Prince Henry become Henry IX, Parliament might well have solved the problem by rigorous economy combined with a thorough overhaul of the system of taxation. As far as we can judge from what we know of young Prince Henry's character, the reign of Henry IX would have been that of a sovereign of the highest character and ability but who would probably have made the English monarchy into an absolutism. Exactly the same thing came about in France in the long reign of Louis XIV. Instead of Henry IX, however, Charles I was the sovereign and his remedy for the troubles of the period was to try to revive all the powers of the Crown which had lapsed or become redundant over the past two hundred years. He surrounded himself, after Buckingham's murder, with men like Archbishop Laud, and the Earl of Strafford, who were excellent servants for an absolute king, but no good to one who had somehow to work with his Parliament.

Despite this bad start, Charles for some eleven years thought himself the happiest king in Europe. He had a brilliant and cultured Court: it was never disgraced by the vile drunkenness and vomitings which had made his father a byword among his own subjects. Charles was also very happy in his domestic life. He had a fine navy, and by reviving many old-forgotten powers he was able to keep going for over ten years without calling a Parliament. Then he had his disaster, war with the Scots over the Prayer Book. He had to call a Parliament. It sat on and off for nearly twenty years and was the instrument of his own execution.

Charles's eldest son, also named Charles, was born and died on 13th May 1629. In the fashion of the time, his next son, born the following year on 29th May, was also called Charles, and lived to inherit his throne as Charles II. Thus the young prince was barely in his teens when the Civil War broke out. The earlier part of his education had followed the now conventional upbringing of a prince who was expected to be versatile in his talents, learned, gay, brilliant and accomplished. It is no unfair commentary on Prince Charles that he who was one of the most intelligent of our kings was also one of the most badly educated. This was not the prince's fault but due simply to his schooling being interrupted. He was never even formally created Prince of Wales, though he held the title, so troubled was the period.

The greatest care had been designed for the education of Prince Charles. He was placed under the management of Cavendish, afterwards Earl of Newcastle, who was to attend to his manners and general upbringing. Cavendish was succeeded by the Marquess of Hertford, and in the seventeenth century a prince even of five years old had his own household and lived quite apart from his parents.

Hertford was succeeded by the Earl of Berkshire. One of the reasons for these frequent changes, all within the space of ten years, was the hostility of the Parliament towards the governors selected by the king for his son and heir. The Parliament wished to have a say in the education of the prince, and it was suggested that John Hampden should be his governor. It is unlikely that anyone could have been found whose name would have been more objectionable to the king and queen as a tutor to their son than Hampden. The king regarded Hampden not only as the leader of the Parliamentary malcontents, but as having caused most of the troubles of the reign. He would not agree to his having anything to do with his son's education. The Parliament retaliated by insisting that Charles should change the tutors of his son. Newcastle was a man who certainly understood one feature of his charge's character, the fact that the boy would learn more from life than from books. "I would not have you too studious," were Newcastle's words to the prince. He sought to train his pupil in outdoor sports, and in love of music. He learned to fence, to dance, and to ride. Charles had also as tutors two men of ability. Hobbes of Malmesbury, who taught him mathematics was at one time an inmate of the Cavendish household, and in him the prince had a tutor of the first rank in scientific and philosophical ability. Thomas Hobbes was one of the great leaders of thought in the age in which he lived; for him to have trained Charles was as though the present Prince of Wales were to receive his mathematical education from Bertrand Russell or science teaching from Julian Huxley.

Charles responded to the training given by Hobbes by retaining a love of scientific problems all his life. He was one of the great encouragers of the Royal Society, and conducted many experiments himself in scientific matters. In other branches of academic education Charles had for tutor Brian Duppa who was eventually Bishop of Winchester. He was much loved by his pupil, but did not instil into him any great care for formal learning. Charles II was noted among the princes of his age as not being too good a Latin scholar.

Charles loved Newcastle, but did not care as much for Hertford and Berkshire. He would, no doubt, have made greater progress in his education had he been able to receive it regularly, but his father's troubles made it impossible for him to study long in any one area. Charles, the prince, was early introduced to problems which Charles, the king, his father, could not solve. The real education of Charles II came through circumstances and events which none could have planned for him. Adversity was his great teacher, and the skill with which he conducted his tenure of the throne was due to the hard lessons he had learnt as a boy. Before he was fourteen Charles had watched the opening battle of the Civil War at Edgehill. He had been left to watch the fight from a safe distance with his tutor for the time, the great Dr. Harvey, the discoverer of the circulation of the blood, and with his younger brother, James. Harvey was more intent upon the book he had brought with him than upon the progress of the fight, and it was not until a cannon ball crashed through the hedge near the little group that Harvey took fright and led his two princes to safety.

From this time on the meetings of prince and king were infrequent and spasmodic. After March 1645 the prince never saw his father again. His mother he had already parted from. The prince was hurried to the west of England. Thence he went into Cornwall, to the Isles of Scilly and to near capture by a Parliamentary fleet. Letters were received from the Parliament asking Charles to come to them, when, said they, everything would be done to render his stay happy and to provide him with every comfort. The prince's advisers rightly distrusted this specious counsel and took the boy away to Jersey. Here he held court and was fêted and admired by the islanders. The Channel Islands were the last part of the realm to hold out for King Charles and when his cause was hopeless everywhere else in the British Isles, it took a determined siege to capture Castle Cornet in Guernsey.

It can be imagined how formative the prince's precarious upbringing was. The troubles of his father's reign were to make him cynical, in due course, to the claims of virtue and consistency. He saw his father opposed by men who prated of virtue and honour, of liberty and public right, but who had no scruples as to the attacks they made on their king. Above all, this type of conduct was seen by the prince to go with a snuffling piety, a Puritanism which he was to grow to detest. The whole bent of what must have been a highly gifted and potentially fine nature was corrupted by the harsh conditions in which he grew to manhood. The name of Charles II is always linked with the names of his famous and infamous mistresses; but apart from his love of women, the other qualities for which he is condemned were due to the harsh school in which he was brought up. He was to say in due time that every man had his price. What more natural when he had had a price placed on his own head? When he saw his life threatened by men who professed themselves as doing God's will?

Charles I and his son parted company in 1645 when the prince was only fifteen. During the four years between this and the king's execution Charles spent his life in wandering over the shrinking area of the royal control—from Oxfordshire to the west of England, then to Scilly and finally to the Channel Isles. His father kept up a correspondence with him, in which he warned the prince never to barter the principles of his regal authority for the sake of preserving the king's life. Charles also gave his son much good advice: the prince was to seek to be remembered as Charles the Good rather than as Charles the Great. He urged his son to learn wisdom from his trials, to adhere to the Church of England, not to strain the law, to use the royal prerogative but not to abuse it; above all, never to leave a promise unperformed. This sage counsel was the fruit of the sad life of Charles I, a life which the king himself had rendered unavoidable by his own actions. Charles also was constantly worried over the possibility of the prince falling into the hands of the Parliament. Well he might be concerned, for the Parliamentary authorities were most anxious to secure control of the heir to the throne. When their invitation to the prince did not work, the Parliament sent a fleet of some twenty sail to capture him in the Scillies. Taking alarm at this move, the friends of the prince took him to Jersey, but neither King Charles nor Queen Henrietta Maria felt secure enough, and from there Prince Charles was hurried to France.

In France the position of Charles was poverty-stricken and unhappy, though his own resilient nature enabled him to enjoy life to some extent. He had little money; the French king would allow him little, and this little was given in charity. Indeed the problem of all exiles was with Charles, that is, how far the government of his country of refuge could afford to recognise and shelter him. Cardinal Mazarin now held sway in France. He continued the policy of his predecessor, Cardinal Richelieu, and maintained friendly relations with the Protestant powers. Mazarin assured the English Parliament that the prince would receive no help from France towards his restoration. The young King, Louis XIV, went with his mother Anne of Austria to visit Charles in the forest of Fontainebleau, and then conducted him to the palace in the forest. The royal revenue of England was of course lost to the queen and the prince. The English exiles who came to be near the exiled royal family also had little money. Most of them had been ruined by their exertions for the king's cause. They brought nothing but wretchedness with them and were a constant reminder of the misery in which the royal cause stood.

Charles felt for his father, who was by now a prisoner of the Parliament, and tried to save him. Nevertheless he did not let his filial feelings entirely interfere with his enjoyment of life. At this time the French Court was diverted, entranced and bewitched by a beautiful and vivacious young coquette, La Grande Mademoiselle, who was of royal birth, the daughter of the wealthy Duke of Orleans. It was the idea of Henrietta Maria to forward a marriage between her son and Mademoiselle de Montpensier. In this scheme the queen was as much moved by considerations of the bride's fortune as by desire for her son to make a match in keeping with his birth. So as soon as he got to France the prince was put forward to make his court to de Montpensier. Strange as it sounds, Charles was tongue-tied in Mademoiselle's presence. He could make little headway. He was, be it remembered, only sixteen and, to make matters worse, he could not speak French, except brokenly—which seems odd, seeing that his mother was French. Mademoiselle was, however, aiming at higher game—Louis XIV, or perhaps the Holy Roman Emperor. Henrietta Maria, notwithstanding, made every effort to secure her fortune for her poor son. At one stage Charles was supposed to be indifferent to the French princess, and so his mother required him to take part in mademoiselle's toilette, which she herself conducted. Charles thus saw the youthful coquette in all her charms being decked for further conquests. Perhaps the young lover had already decided that the woman whom he required was not a coquette but one with more human qualities. His suit to the Grande Mademoiselle did not prosper, and probably just as well.

The dream of a marriage with the great French heiress was eventually broken by the dire news of the king's death. Charles, at the end of 1648, had taken command of a Parliamentary fleet which had revolted off the coast of Holland, and had sailed for England in order to bring about the saving of his father's life. The demonstration failed, however, and Charles returned without action. Then, after this, the prince sent to England a paper blank save for his signature, so that Parliament might put therein their own conditions as long as his father's life was saved. There was no response to this. The Parliamentarians were bent on Charles I's death. When the news came to Prince Charles he could hardly credit it. He had probably never thought that the execution would be carried out. When he recovered from the shock of his father's death, he further realized that the title he held—King Charles II—might well prove a hopeless and useless one. The only ray of hope came from Scotland. The Scots having sold the father, now decided that they would be patronizingly loyal to the son. He was invited to go to Scotland, and to become king provided he would take the Solemn Covenant and subscribe to rule as the Kirk directed. His fortunes were so hopeless that he agreed for even a throne on the harsh conditions offered by the Scots was better than nothing. He soon found the Scots the hardest of masters. His woman-loving nature could not possibly escape censure from the godly ministers, who, backed up by Biblical precepts, opposed kings and preached against great ones. Charles had to sit on the penitence stool, to listen to rude and offensive sermons, and to suffer Kirk discipline.

Charles was now twenty-one and already his mistress, Lucy Waters, had borne him the unlucky Duke of Monmouth, James Crofts as he was called. To such a prince the rigid rules of the Kirk had no appeal, and Charles's life was unhappy in the extreme. He must have been glad when the time came for him to seek relief in action. Dunbar was fought and the Scots were beaten; then came the long march and dash into England, when Charles fought a hard battle against Cromwell and his army. For four hours the Cavaliers contended with the Ironsides, and when the battle was lost Charles wished to die in the fighting rather than be a king in hiding. Return to Scotland was out of the question, even had he wished to try out the loyalty of the Scots to a king in defeat. By shifts and turns, aided by men and women of all degrees, often poor people, the defeated king made his way to France. A large sum was put on the head of the young man, Charles Stuart, as the Roundheads called him. Yet, through thick and thin, ordinary folk stood by him, and safely he evaded the Round-heads and got to France. He was not allowed to remain in France. Cromwell's Government became influential in Europe and the crowned heads could not afford to let the wishes of Cromwell be disregarded. Charles was thus forced to leave France and to wander through the Low Countries. To Spa, and to Cologne, to the Rhineland and Holland he went. For nearly ten years his lot was that of a wandering exile. One cannot help reflecting that the fate which has overtaken several great royalties of Europe in our own time should also have very nearly befallen the British monarchy three hundred years ago. During the exile the Cromwellian or Republican Government passed through a series of experiments in various forms of rule to (as usually happens in revolutions) a return to authoritarian rule. Cromwell, as is well known, wished at one time to have the title of king and to transmit the throne in his own family. But when the weary nation had been forced to undergo everything from wild democracy to strict tyranny, it turned willingly enough to its ancient form of rule. God save King Charles II was the heartfelt cry of all but a tiny minority. All was made ready to unthread the rude eye of rebellion and to conduct the still youthful sovereign to his throne. When that sovereign, now thirty years old, lay down in the Whitehall palace of his predecessors, he was resolved never to travel again. He was an experienced man of the world, one who had certainly fulfilled the desire of his first governor, to learn from life rather than from books. The education of the Prince of Wales had been in a very hard school, but the pupil proved apt.

Charles II left a numerous progeny but no legitimate child. His brother, James, Duke of York, who succeeded him as James II, seemed likely to share the same misfortune. He had had four sons by his first wife, of whom none lived long. He married again, to Mary of Modena, and a son, named Charles, styled like his dead half-brothers (three of them) Duke of Cambridge, died in the year of his birth, 1677. In 1688 the growing tyranny of James II was made tolerable for the Protestants by the thought that he had no children to take his place on the throne. Then a rumour grew of the queen's expecting another child. On 10th June 1688 the queen gave birth to a prince, James Francis Edward. This was the child of whom the Protestants and adherents of the House of Hanover wished to believe that he was not James's child at all, but a boy smuggled into the palace in a warming-pan. It was a ridiculous fable; there were many people present at the time of the prince's birth, including the Lords of the Privy Council. Nonetheless the rumour that the prince was not genuine gathered strength from the desire that James should not be succeeded by a Papist son. It was during the early months of the prince's life that intrigues were going on, in which most of the great men and noble families in England were implicated, to replace James by his nephew, William of Orange, on the English throne. The birth of James Francis Edward was a peculiarly awkward stumbling-block for those who wished to put away James II. The king, for his part, was well aware of the powers gathering against him and his house. As if to counteract this, he early gave his son the title of Prince of Wales,

Frederick Lewis, Prince of Wales, 1727: died before his father, George II.

George William, Prince of Wales, 1751 : afterwards George III.

for at the boy's baptism on 15th October he was described as H.R.H. the Prince of Wales. On 11th December James II was in flight from England, and was held by his Parliament to have abdicated the throne. James, naturally, disputed this, but the hard fact was that he had to leave the country and take his family with him. The exiled royalty, again, took refuge in the France of Louis XIV. Now, however, the King of France was a ruler in his own right. He wished to give asylum to his brother monarch, and do so he would, despite anything that the new Government in England might declare. There in France at St. Germains the Court of James II re-formed, and soon a sister was born to the Prince of Wales. The child soon became acquainted with hard tidings. James II set out for Ireland, the only part of his dominions which seemed willing to welcome him, but where his cause was soon overthrown. Back at St. Germains, the king had to reconcile himself to a dreary exile, hoping that one day the English people would recall him. In 1701 he died, just before his nephew, the former Prince of Orange, William III of England. Then in 1702, Anne, James's daughter by his first wife, came to the throne. She was half-sister of the exiled James VII and III as the Jacobites called him. The boy, who was then only fourteen, had been brought up in the Catholic religion and with the political views of his father, so that he had little chance of gaining the throne. Had he been able to do as Henry IV of France, and adopt a religion in which he had no faith, but felt it necessary to accept, he could, quite possibly, have become King of England, Scotland and Ireland, for it was on the score of the religion that the English people objected to the Stuarts. But James Francis Edward was a devout Catholic and so remained throughout his life. At twelve he went in great state to Notre Dame to make his first communion, and a medal was struck for presentation to the Royalists. At fourteen he was proclaimed King of England at St. Germains, but he had not an acre of Britain which he could call his own.

France continued to protect the young titular king and his mother, and both waited for the hour, which must surely come, when they would be recalled. Indeed, some of the Scots lords came to ask James to visit Scotland where they were sure that the old hatred of the English would make him welcome and ensure a rising in his favour. The Glorious Revolution of 1688 had been made in England, and the Scots were not apt to take their southern neighbours' actions with any loving feeling. The exiled queen would not let the young boy prince-king go, and so a good chance was lost. Then, again, in 1707 or 1708, a chance came which he did seize, and he sailed for Scotland, only to be turned back by a British fleet. It was this incident which Sir Walter Scott mentioned at the end of *The Black Dwarf*. At last came a chance in 1714, when Queen Anne died, and the Elector of Hanover, who understood little if any English, was to be invited over to be king. The English supporters of the young Stuart prince-king bungled the matter and failed at the last moment. Had they proclaimed him king on the death of his half-sister he would most likely have succeeded without much trouble. But they lost their chance and the prince went to Scotland, where he did no more than sight the coast, for the clans, although victorious at Sheriffmuir, were not sufficiently united to make a regular stand against the Government forces and the 1715 rebellion petered out. George I was firmly seated on his throne. James returned to France.

By the supporters of Hanover he was styled the Pretender. A way had to be found for men of good manners to refer to him without upsetting each other's feelings and convictions. He was termed the Chevalier de St. George. With that title he had to be content for all his long life. He died in 1766 at the age of seventy-eight, after having seen three kings of the Hanoverian line mount his throne, and after two full-scale attempts had been made and failed in his favour. He had married, in 1719, Clementina, a Polish princess and grand-daughter of John Sobieski, King of Poland. By her he had two sons, Charles Edward and Henry. The elder of these was a gallant youth, who at the age of twenty-five went to Scotland and landed there with six men. Gathering the clans around him, this titular Prince of Wales went in a few months from despair to triumph and back to despair again. At first he drove all before him. He won the battle of Prestonpans, and appeared to have subdued Scotland. Evading the armies sent against him, he marched into England, and marched as far as Derby, where the failure of the English Jacobites to join him compelled his advisers to realize the terrible risks of the expedition, and forced him to return to Scotland. On the retreat he won another battle at Falkirk, but the net was closing round him, and his area of manœuvre grew smaller. At Culloden Moor he faced irretrievable disaster, and his forces were scattered. Terrible retribution was taken against the Highland tribes, of the sort which they often meted out to each other. Charles was in hiding like his great uncle after Worcester, and a price of £30,000 was put on his head. Yet he, too, found faithful friends and escaped to the Continent. The Stuart cause was finished. James III (to give him the empty title) had been compelled to leave France and to live in Italy. Here the last titular Stuart Prince of Wales dragged out his inglorious life. The months spent campaigning in Scotland had been Charles Edward's hour of glory; and his later life made many regret that he had not fallen, as he had wished, at Culloden. Drunkenness and debauchery filled up his days, and known to all by the poor title of "king in exile", he had scarcely any friends. Sir Walter Scott in one of his most charming works, *Redgauntlet*, treats the legend that Charles Edward was once more in Britain as a fact. However this may be, the Stuart agents could not work up any more enthusiasm for their master. He had no friends among the European Governments. He had no heirs—legitimate, that is. When he died he was succeeded by his younger brother, Henry, who had embraced religion and had risen to be a cardinal of the Roman Church. Henry contented himself with the title of Henry IX and added on his medals, *voluntate Dei non hominum*. Henry did not repine over his lot but lived happily as a Prince of the Church. When the French Revolution affected Italy, Henry, Cardinal York, found his revenues seriously diminished, and was glad to accept a pension from his cousin, George III. In receipt of that generous help, he died in 1805, and with him died the last of the Stuart line and the last flicker of the Stuart cause, if flicker it could be called. By the princely care of George IV, the two Stuarts, Charles Edward and Henry, were commemorated with their father in the church of St. Peter's at Rome. So ended the inglorious story of the exiled line, with its two titular Princes of Wales. The conflicting forces which had made them exiles had also caused an enormous transformation in the position of the royal family in this country and in the education and preparation of the heir to the throne.

CHAPTER X

The Princes of Hanover

THE Hanoverian dynasty is perhaps the most interesting
royal line in our history with the exception of the house
of Tudor, and probably more interesting even than the
Tudors from the constitutional point of view. It has been under
the rule of the House of Hanover that the greatest changes
in the history of Britain have taken place. The monarchy
itself from their advent has changed very greatly, a change
which is summed up in the phrase that the sovereign reigns
but does not rule. Yet this momentous change has been the
result, not of carefully laid plan but almost of accident.

Nothing is more curious in the history of the English
monarchy than the choice of sovereigns. After the expulsion
of James II the English people were voluntarily under the rule
of foreign sovereigns, with the exception of Queen Anne, for
nearly one hundred years. William of Orange was willing to
undertake the government of England as part of his great
design of building up opposition to Louis XIV. William never
minded the criticism of his English subjects because he already
had a royal title which was his by birth and not conferred by
any Parliament. He brought a Dutch army with him and to
Dutchmen were confided the strong places of his kingdom and
the security of his person. It was a curious contradiction in a
people who had so strongly objected to the Irish troops whom
James II had employed. Still, the Dutchmen were Protestants.

Protestantism: that is the key to the otherwise very strange
and, to outward view, unpatriotic behaviour of the English.
The King of England by hereditary right, James II, could have
remained on his throne, whatever his misbehaviour and his
cruelties, if only he had the good sense of Henry IV of France

and had preferred the Book of Common Prayer to the Mass. It was not the harsh treatment which he meted out to the countrymen following Monmouth which drove James's people into revolt against him, but the fear that he was going to make England again a Roman Catholic country.

It was the need to preserve the national Protestantism which made the alliance between Church of England and Free Churchmen against James's specious tolerance. It was the need to preserve Protestantism which made Englishmen welcome to their country's throne a man who could not speak a word of English and who had no liking for England, who manifestly preferred Hanover to the land which had made him a king. It was the refusal to abjure Rome which made the cause of the Pretenders, father and son alike, hopeless, whatever transient gleams of success might gild their arms at first.

Despite the changes which replaced a native by a foreign-speaking sovereign, the bulk of the people of England and of Britain remained loyal to the crown. There were to be plenty of instances in the nineteenth century of Balkan countries taking as their kings the scions of some German or Germanic house. These kings had need to tread warily if they wished to reign without fear. Yet the Elector of Hanover, when he came to rule in England, was really in the same position as these Balkan sovereigns were to be in the next century. However, no Hanoverian sovereign was ever afraid of his subjects, except possibly George IV when he had his matrimonial differences brought out into the light of day. George I and George II, both essentially foreigners, behaved as though they were the rulers of England by hereditary right, as in theory they were. They had been brought in because the heirs with a prior right to the throne had adopted a belief which did not appeal to the majority of English people. Therefore the Hanoverians should have been fairly amenable, constitutional sovereigns. In fact they were nothing of the sort.

Radical constitutional changes are reckoned from the time (1714) when the Elector of Hanover became George I. True, there were great changes in the relationship between governed and governor, but these came about almost as the result of chance. It might have been thought that, after having killed one king and exiled another, the English would have been most truculent to the new occupants of the throne. Yet far from it; the Court which surrounded the Georges was as sycophantic and fawning as the most absolute Stuart could have desired. Not only the Court, but the Government, the Houses of Parliament, all who were connected with the Crown, were all full of deference to the new rulers.

That being so, it might again have been supposed that the education of the heir to the throne would be conducted on the same lines as of old—that he would be represented on every council of importance, early be initiated into state business and would almost automatically act as regent should his father be out of the kingdom.

Nothing of the sort happened. It is from the era of the Hanoverians that we date the change in the education of the Prince of Wales, from which we are only just now beginning to recover. The reason for this change is, that for some reason not adequately explained the kings from Hanover hated their eldest sons, and desired to keep them from occupying any place of power or responsibility until it should prove impossible to avoid doing so. Whereas Henry V had been President of the Council at twenty, and the Black Prince even before that age had been nominally regent of the country for his absent father, the Princes of Wales of the House of Hanover were never allowed to have public employment.

What was the cause of this phenomenon, that father and son should be in enmity? According to some, it was due to jealousy of the father for the son, and fear that the son's popularity would jeopardise the father's position. The idea of abdication or perhaps of retirement to Hanover, with the loss of English revenues, always inspired the reigning sovereign to fear and hate his heir.

All sorts of theories have been devised to explain this feature of the Hanoverian dynasty, but none are satisfactory probably because it was psychologically peculiar to that royal line.

The origin of the Hanoverian claim to the English throne was, like most dynastic claims, tangled. James I's eldest daughter, Elizabeth, married the Elector Palatine of the Rhine, who became King of Bohemia. They had a numerous family, the famous Prince Rupert of the Rhine being one of them. The youngest daughter, Sophia, married Ernest Augustus, Duke of Brunswick Luneburg, Elector of Hanover. Sophia expected to succeed Queen Anne, but the ailing queen managed to outlive her cousin of Hanover by a couple of months. Then, under the Act of Settlement, the son of Sophia and the Elector became King of England. He was George Lewis, Elector of Hanover.

The new king lost no time in coming to claim his good fortune. He was accompanied by a formidable crowd of persons from Hanover who came with only one object—to make their fortunes. In this many of them were successful. George I, as we may now call him, had with him two of his mistresses, ladies named respectively Schulenberg and Kilmasegge. Countess Platen was left behind, on the grounds that as she was a Catholic her religion might upset the English. It was not felt that her profession of royal whore would unduly irritate George's new Protestant subjects. George I was also accompanied by his Prime Minister and various other officials from Hanover, plus his personal attendants, two Turks, Mustafa and Mahomet, who had been taken captive by him during his campaigns against the Turks. In fact, the new king brought a ready-made court with him. His interest in his new realm was strictly on a business footing. It represented to him the opportunity of getting more power and money. Anyone who thinks that the arrival of George I in England heralded the time when the British sovereign was respectful to his ministers should study the reign of George I. His bargains with his ministers resulted in a payment to him of one million pounds a year. This is more than the royal allowance in 1958 (more by half), and it was in the more valuable money of 1714.

The new king's main idea was to reward those who had followed him from the glories of Hanover to the terrible country of England. His two Protestant mistresses he made life peeresses. Thus the life peerage has undoubtedly interesting and colourful precedence. Ermengarde Melusina, Baroness von der Schulenberg, was made (for life) Duchess of Munster, with other titles. She also received the Duchy of Kendal. Nor was George deterred by English scruples from remembering his Catholic mistress. Countess von Platen was created Countess of Leinster, Countess of Darlington and Baroness Brentford.

It can easily be understood that a king whose outlook on life was so manifestly concerned with material things would not be likely to be a very good influence on the education of his heir. George I was accompanied by his son, George Augustus. The king's first act in his new Council was the creation of his heir as Prince of Wales. Any idea that here was a fond father hastening to bestow new honours on the apple of his eye can be abandoned. George was advised by his ministers that the heir to the throne was always given the title of Prince of Wales. He therefore acted on this advice, probably reflecting also that, to support the new dignity of prince for his heir, more money would be required—which would, of course, go through his own hands first.

Father and son cordially detested one another. To George I the existence of George Augustus was a perpetual reminder of a wife whom he also detested, the unfortunate Sophia Dorothea, the only daughter of the Duke of Brunswick and Zelle. George had been married to her in 1682. In 1694 they were divorced, and she was imprisoned in a castle for her infidelity. She died in 1726, only a year before her husband. She thus spent more than thirty years in captivity, and her son, George Augustus, was never again allowed to see her. Parted from his mother at the age of eleven, George Augustus never forgot her, and made several attempts to see her again, but never succeeded. Had his mother survived his father, George Augustus meant to bring her to England.

George I, therefore, strove to slight the Prince of Wales in every way. There were perpetual quarrels between them. Even at the christening of the prince's child, George William, Duke of Gloucester, a fracas broke out. The prince wished to have royal sponsors for his child's baptism. The king wished to have the Duke and Duchess of Newcastle. The prince understood that these two were to act as proxies for the absent royal godparents. When he discovered that the Newcastles were to be godparents in reality, the prince could not control himself. He called the Duke of Newcastle a rascal, and threatened him. The result was a breach of the peace in the very presence of the sovereign. George I was secretly delighted. He ordered the Prince of Wales to be arrested and confined to his chambers. The English ministers were horrified by this, and succeeded in talking the king round to the extent that he agreed to remove the guard from the prince's person. However, the king then proceeded to give the prince notice to quit. He had to leave all the royal palaces, and his princess was to follow him as soon as she had recovered from the effects of childbirth. No one was to consort with the prince if the king could prevent it. This was in 1717 and was a lively beginning to the new reign.

It was with considerable difficulty that the prince found accommodation, but eventually he and the Princess of Wales set up home at Leicester House, where a kind of alternative court was formed. The king found a Whig government in power when he came to the throne. In those days the Ministry was associated with the sovereign. The king could not read the usual Gracious Speech at the opening of his first Parliament, his command of English being insufficient for the purpose, so it was read for him by one of his ministers. The Tories were out of office, having played their cards very badly over the last days of Queen Anne and having failed to support the exiled Stuarts while at the same time not going out strongly enough for the incoming Hanoverians.

In consequence of the king having a Whig Ministry the prince sought out the Tories. Some Whigs also clove to him, and Leicester House parties became very much the vogue. The king made it clear that no one who went to Leicester House would be received at Court. Nonetheless many went, and a new party began to gather around the prince, who would be king in the not too distant future. (George I was fifty-four when he succeeded to the throne.)

There were thus two rival courts in London. Every so often the prince went through a form of reconciliation with his father. This usually had its rise in the necessity to obtain money. Nothing could make the king like the prince, but when one of the king's lords, Lord Berkeley, First Lord of the Admiralty, suggested that the prince should be abducted from England, the king did not agree with the amiable suggestion. As, however, he kept the document containing the proposition, he obviously did not discountenance the idea. Had he been able safely to defy public opinion there is little doubt that he would have agreed to Berkeley's suggestion.

The trouble between father and son was aggravated by the popularity of the prince. The boy had early shown himself eager, as the man was later, to be the champion of England. When he reached his new country he was full of praise for everything he saw, and he declared himself an Englishman. He was soon popular with his future subjects, and he did everything he could to ingratiate himself with them.

George I's persecution of the prince went to the extraordinary extent of making an attempt to gain legal control of the prince's children. On this point a strenuous controversy raged. The case was put to the judges of England, who were obviously in a very difficult position because of the king's power to hinder their promotion or to remove them from office, as in the case of the Lord Chancellor. Still, there were some judges independent enough to give the opinion that the father of the children had the right to determine where they should live and the mode of their education. The rest of the Bench decided that the king's authority was absolute in the education of his grandchildren. However, the children continued to live with their parents.

Three main features distinguish all the Hanoverian kings and their heirs from other dynasties of Kings of England. One, and perhaps the most important, was the mutual dislike of father and son. This seemed to be inherent and could hardly be ascribed in every instance to the father's fear of his son usurping him, as Henry IV had obviously feared in the case of Prince Hal. This hateful feature of the new royal family continued under good kings such as George III, as well as under such disreputable characters as George I and II. It even continued on into the reign of Queen Victoria, for there was certainly a gulf, if not hostility, between Prince Albert, the Prince Consort, and his heir, the future King Edward VII. All writers agree that a difference of view and liking, which I think is a fairly safe way of describing it, existed between Victoria and Edward, and some writers, with considerable show of reason, ascribe it to dislike on the part of the mother. In fact, this very unpleasant trait did not pass out of the royal family until the happy era of King Edward VII and his sons.

The second feature of the Hanoverian dynasty in the relations of the Prince of Wales was the refusal of the sovereign to allow his heir to have any real political education. I have striven to show in these pages that the real education of the Princes of Wales did not end with their formal studies which were more concentrated and partook of more heaviness than entertainment than those of other young men of noble family. The education of a Prince of Wales right up to the Hanoverian succession was automatically understood to include a deliberate understudying of his father's position. Edward II had to preside over the Great Council and the Parliament during his father's absence. Indeed, on one occasion at least it was thought better that the "Lord Edward" should preside rather than Edward I, as at that time the king was passing through a phase of difficult relations with his baronage.

The Black Prince had been appointed the guardian of England at the age of eight. Naturally, the real work was confided to his elders, but from that tender age the boy was expected to understand the procedure of Parliaments and councils. In view of this, it is not surprising that Henry V should have been President of the Council at twenty. The training of the heir apparent demanded that he should be able to step into his father's place, not only when he succeeded in the order of nature but when the father's absence or preoccupation required it. It is true that Henry IV removed his son from the position of Council President, but this was due to a conscience-stricken usurper's fear of being dethroned by his own son. Unfortunately this was the only precedent in the matter of the political education of Princes of Wales which Queen Victoria could recall when her son asked for employment. Moreover, she thought the great king of Agincourt had been dismissed for incompetence.

Under the Tudors and Stuarts the same kind of practical training went on. Prince Arthur had been sent down to Wales to govern the principality through the Council of Wales at Ludlow. Prince Henry, his brother, though not then the immediate heir to the throne, had been carefully trained to take office in state or church in due course. Few would query the very rough but extremely effective political educations of the Princesses Mary and Elizabeth. Prince Henry, son of James I, had been concerned with the Navy when he sat in the Council; he died ere he was nineteen. Charles I was, of course, used to various employments before he came to the throne. That he did not profit by them was due to the wrong twist given to his education by James and Buckingham.

There was, therefore, between the Hanoverians and their predecessors a complete breach in the upbringing of the heir apparent. His formal education became more severe. The curriculum laid down for several of the Hanoverian princes seems to envisage a king ruling over a large territory peopled by the inhabitants of Lamaseries. Apart from his natural mental affliction, George III's troubles seem to have stemmed from the fact that though not inadequately educated in the academic sense, he knew little of life when called to rule. The course of study laid down for Edward VII was sufficiently hard to prompt verses in periodicals such as *Punch* which were far more intrusive into the affairs of the royal family than most of what, in popular newspapers, is complained of today.

Yes, formal education got much harder but the practical training of one who must in the order of nature rule a growing empire was neglected. From 1714, when the Hanoverians started their career as kings of Britain, there is hardly an instance of an heir apparent being given a job to do, apart from the everlasting laying of foundation stones and being the recipient of illuminated addresses.

The third distinguishing feature of the Hanoverian dynasty is of an altogether most unpleasant character. Few people with knowledge of the world are surprised at stories of the unchastity of princes in history. The usual excuse is that they have to marry to please others and not themselves, and hence their taking of mistresses. This is not the whole story. Princes have usually had more time, more opportunity and more to offer to a woman than the bulk of their subjects. They therefore tended in times past at least to have more attachments than others. Illegitimate children are often mentioned in the chronicles of the Kings of England. When few or none are mentioned, it is a matter for wonder at the king's virtue or moderation.

Granted all this, it remains a fact that few of our kings have made their vices disgusting or revolting. This achievement was to be reserved for the Hanoverian kings. The favourite practice of George I and George II was to place their reigning mistress in attendance upon their queens. With them all, George II, and his son Frederick (the Prince of Wales, who never reigned but was father of George III), and George IV, debauchery had no gildings of taste or refinement: George I, on the day of his wife's death (admittedly he had been parted from her for a generation, and on the score of infidelity), went to the theatre to sit between two of his mistresses.

George II was genuinely fond of Queen Caroline. Indeed it is not too much to say that he was devoted to her. He used to discuss his lady friends with her rather as a modern man might go over his crossword with his wife. The queen, for her part, appeared sympathetic and interested and took the new favourite into her household, but it was said that by so doing she was able to keep an eye on the mistress, and to see that she did not extend her power into the king's cabinet.

There was no graceful gallantry about the affairs of George I, George II or the Prince Regent. There was no inhibition about lies or other unworthy conduct if the royal sinner felt they were necessary. The truth was, the Hanoverians brought a Germanic strain into our affairs, and a complete disregard for the older English traditions.

It is possible to be tolerant about the affairs of Charles II, and few people are disgusted by them; but it is not only the strait-laced who object to the behaviour of the Georges. Their amours disgust by their grossness. This quality is reflected in the very free attitude taken up by the newspapers and books of the period. The Prime Minister once (in the time of George II) described the king's lady friend by a term now used more in the language of the streets. Lampoons are found with reference to the physical behaviour of the sovereign even with his queen. In one so-called poem George II, after a stormy crossing from Hanover, was said "to ride at large in Carolina's arms". On another occasion a notice was put up outside the palace describing a man (the king having gone to Hanover) who had left his wife and six children on the parish. Once a broken-down cart and horse was put out parading the streets with an inscription to the effect that this was the equipage designed to fetch George and his whore from Hanover.

These three qualities combined to render the Hanoverian dynasty very untrue to form compared with earlier dynasties. To many people today looking back it seems that 1714 saw the arrival of a new type of monarchy. And elementary history books teach that the Hanoverians were the first truly constitutional monarchs: that right up to the end of the seventeenth century the country, for good or ill, depended to a large extent upon the character of its sovereigns. Then came the change and we went in for Parliaments and parties, and Prime Ministers and so on. This is an agreeable theory; but the greater the study given to it, the less it is agreeable to facts.

The loyalty of the English people to the principle of monarchy has always been much greater than their dislike of a particular sovereign. It has recently been suggested that the abdication of the Duke of Windsor sorely strained the monarchical feelings of the people. I do not think so. Whether we look back to olden days or look at more modern times, we find that monarchy has always been able to keep round it such an aura that the worst sovereign has been able to count on support from a large section of his people. It confounds belief that a creature as bad as Ethelred the Unready should still have commanded respect. It is astonishing that England's greatest poet should have composed a patriotic play about England's worst king (as popularly conceived).

When the last male Stuart left the country a Dutchman took the throne, albeit with an English consort. Nonetheless the Dutchman reigned after her death and was not in danger of being dethroned. Then came Anne. After her death the line of native-born sovereigns ended. The English hastened to transfer their allegiance to a king who could speak no English, cared little for England, and only wanted the wealth of the country for himself.

Then when the king was a German, unable to comprehend the language of his new realm and not wanting to understand its customs, no frantic scramble was made for power over the monarch. The Cabinet began to sit without him, but he was identified in the popular mind with his ministers, and their policy was his. As proof of this, in each Georgian reign a party gathered round the heir apparent and made ready for the day when he should mount the throne. Of course, if the king's party were Whigs, Tories formed the bulk of the Prince of Wales's party. Every now and then, for the sake of public appearances, the king, on the advice of his ministers, would go through the farce of a reconciliation with his heir. At the first court holden thereafter the king would be surrounded by his courtiers, while the Prince of Wales at the other end of the room would have his future court in embryo around him. It was all very unedifying, especially when ministers found out that an apparently friendly move on the king's part was really the stalking horse to obtain more than his fair share of the prince's income as voted by Parliament.

One million pounds a year was the bargain which George wrung out of his new country. The Prince of Wales had to be content with £50,000 until the Commons insisted on doubling it, when the king thought he was going to get a grip on the extra money. But for once the usually dutiful Commons stood firm and the prince got the full income.

Certainly there is nothing in the behaviour of the German kings which warrants the idea that they were humble clients of Parliament. For one thing, the king of this land is not supposed to leave it without permission or consent of the Government; but when thePrime Minister trie dto explain this to George I he met with a blank refusal to listen and the king went off to his beloved Hanover. In fact, the German kings made it perfectly clear that they valued Hanover far above England, and England as merely the means to enjoy a more ample life in Hanover. Little wonder that there were insurrections in Scotland and even in northern England. Yet, although the Scots rabble had little use for a king who never showed himself in Scotland (between Charles II and George IV no sovereign ever did), they cared as little for their ancient Stuart line. Only

Edward Albert, Prince of Wales, 1911. As Edward VIII abdicated
December, 1936. H.R.H. The Duke of Windsor.

The Investiture of the Prince of Wales at Caernarvon Castle, 1911. Presentation at the King's Gate.

Caernarvon Castle, 1911. The Prince of Wales reading the declaration.

a few thousands rose in arms for the Pretenders in 1715 and 1745, and the great bulk of those few were Highlanders.

But this is to digress. The younger man could in the ordinary course of events afford to bide his time. George I knew that his son must eventually take his place, but during his life he kept his heir from any but the most indirect knowledge of affairs, and refused him employment, even refusing him his right to be a soldier. George, Prince of Wales was kept from the army until he came to the throne. Then he proved his courage by being the last English king to lead his men into battle. At Dettingen he showed his mettle; and the worst enemy of the Hanoverians could not describe them as cowards.

After the accession of the second George to the throne, his behaviour towards his heir was, if anything, worse than that of his father towards him. Frederick, Prince of Wales was not destined to come to the throne, and if his end could have been hastened by malignity, then his father and mother would have been among his murderers. Neither George II nor Queen Caroline could endure the presence of Frederick, their eldest. Yet they were affectionate, as far as they could be, to their other children. When they were with Frederick they affected not to see him except when forced to address some formal remark to him. Vile language was used about him by his parents; he was described as fool, sot and impotent ass. His ability to produce an heir was cast into doubt in the worst and most public language. Why he should have been treated in this way cannot now be discovered. It was certainly a most extreme example of bitter hostility of father to son.

Frederick, Prince of Wales disappointed the hopes of those who had gathered round him by dying, before his father, in 1751. His father said of him when alive: "My dear first born is the greatest ass, and the greatest liar, and the greatest canaille, and the greatest beast in the whole world, and I heartily wish he was out of it." When the prince was dead, George II while at cards, remarked casually on the fact and went on with the game.

Frederick himself might have broken the evil spell had he lived to see his own son George (afterwards George III). He left behind him a testament for George which reads not only wisely but lovingly. At any rate, the hostility of George II for his heir was never prolonged into the generation of his grandchildren. George was fond of his grandson, though he did not bother much with the boy's education. This was left entirely to his mother and her friends. As a result, the future George III had the worst education of anyone who has been formally prepared for the throne in England. He was created Prince of Wales very soon after his father's death, and his governors, as they were called, were appropriate to his station but subordinate to his mother.

The opinion given by one of these governors, Lord Waldegrave, was not flattering to the royal pupil. Among other defects he saw that the prince would often mistake wrong for right and would then be obstinate in adhering to his views. He sulked on occasion and was moody. On the score of formal education Lord Waldegrave did not hesitate to pronounce it bad. He said that the tutors had been good and learned men but had been overborne by the royal mother.

It is not hard to see the defects of the future George III in this account. He had little equipment from his education to counter the faults of his character. The lesson most frequently given to him came from his mother with her exhortations, "George, be a king!"

The mother had a favourite, Lord Bute, and the vulgar did not hesitate to ascribe moral failings to their relationship: Bute was supposed to be lover of the Princess of Wales. It was not until after George became king that Bute ceased to exercise influence.

There were many rumours about the marriage which George was supposed to have made with Hannah Lightfoot, a Quakeress, which if true would have invalidated the subsequent marriage with Charlotte of Mecklenburg Strelitz. There were so many discrepancies in the accounts of this story that probably little notice was taken of them because they were so manifestly ridiculous and false. They may have had behind them the substance of a youthful affair, but nothing more. The problem of royal marriage was to occupy George's attention in future years but for a very different reason than this supposed early misdemeanour.

Under George III kingly rule certainly remained a fact, and many would add that the disastrous failure of the king's policy towards the American colonies showed the dangers of such rule. With respect to those who think so it does nothing of the sort. The king was right, at the very beginning, in asking the American colonists to pay their share of the expenses incurred for their defence in the Seven Years War. There is some truth in Chesterton's verses about freedom from French attack making it safe to indulge in dreams of democracy and freedom.

On grounds of expediency the king was probably wrong to persist in his American policy, but, even so had he not been unlucky in his military operations he might have won the war. Had the war been prosecuted thoroughly from the start, had General Burgoyne been able to meet his colleagues as arranged, the Americans, instead of winning Saratoga, would have been annihilated. Then again, had Robert Clive been despatched to America he would most likely have brought the lucky touch, so much desired by Napoleon among a general's qualities, to the war.

The American war failed, however, and the king has been saddled with the blame of losing the American colonies. It is always said that the last time an English king intervened in politics disaster followed. It would be much truer to say that the last English king who played a decisive part in politics failed because his mind gave way.

The hostile relations of the earlier Georges with their heirs were reproduced between George III and his eldest son, George. There was a great difference in character between George III and his grandfather, and at last grossness had passed out of the royal court. Yet the Hanoverian characteristics were present just as they had been fifty years earlier and as they were to be a century later. Mention is often made of the sixty years' tenure of the position of Prince of Wales by Edward VII, but it is often forgotten that nearly the same length of time passed for the future George IV as Prince of Wales.

George, afterwards Prince Regent and George IV, was born in 1762, and declared Prince of Wales at five days old. This was at an even younger age than Edward VII who became Prince of Wales at a month old. The new prince did not succeed to the throne until he was fifty-eight years old. With the exception of the period from 1811 to 1820 he never held any power. During that time he was Prince Regent. Yet even in 1811–1820 he could not exercise proper power because by the time he reached the position of Prince Regent he was forty-nine and had long exhausted his credit with the nation.

The life of George IV is a reminder of the folly of bad education. He was not essentially a bad man, and in his youth was handsome, slim, accomplished, popular and witty. He asked repeatedly for employment, especially of the martial variety. He lived in an age when any Englishman who had courage, good health and some ability had the chance of glory under leaders of heroic stature, like Nelson and Wellington. Had the Prince of Wales been allowed to imitate his brothers and adopt a military career, in reality he might have made a name for himself, and been admired by his people. Every request for martial status was refused by the king, and so likewise was his every attempt to gain knowledge of the workings of state. How would a managing director of a great business train his destined successor? Surely by initiating him in an increasing degree to business responsibilities. But such a common-sense course was ruled out of the question with the infinitely more important affairs of a great empire.

With the avenues to public life firmly closed to him, George, Prince of Wales sought out pleasure. He became the first Gentleman in Europe. He found a diversion in architecture.

He took the lead in clothes and fashionable amusement. He took affairs of the heart very seriously. He pursued an actress, Mrs. Robinson, who was renowned for her part as Perdita in Shakespeare's *Tempest*. The prince wrote notes to her under the name of Florizel. Eventually she became the prince's mistress and a child was born of the liaison. The affair did not last long, and there followed many other Perditas throughout the prince's life. A stream of females passed along the corridors of George's career, and he made himself more than ever ridiculous with each new conquest. The only real love of his life was Mrs. FitzHerbert. The story of their affairs has been told many times. To many they were husband and wife. They did, indeed, go through a marriage ceremony on 15th

December 1785, and Mrs. FitzHerbert believed herself to be his wife. In fact, in law, they could not have been legally married because the Royal Marriages Act of 1772 required the consent of the sovereign to the marriage of his children.

The darker features in the prince's character came out after his marriage to Mrs. FitzHerbert. He soon began to treat her in a disgraceful manner, to conduct affairs with other women. Moreover, his extravagance grew ever greater. His debts mounted vastly. He could only be rescued from his predicament by a marriage in accordance with his father's wishes. His income was £63,000 per year, and he was given £30,000 to settle his debts and a further £30,000 to set up his establishment in Carlton House. Unfortunately, he was enabled by his position as heir to the throne to enjoy credit on promises to pay when he became king. Soon after the settlement just mentioned the prince's debts were £250,000.

In 1789 the king had one of his mental relapses, which seemed to promise George an early accession to the throne. Yet his conduct had been so bad that he had lost most of his real friends and he was not trusted by the nation at large. So although the king's illness incapacitated him from dealing with affairs of state, the prince could be regent only in name. He could not grant appointments, create peers, or bestow honours, or control the royal property. Had he objected, then his mother and not he would have been made regent.

The prince had not hesitated to tell lies to extricate himself from any difficult position. He had followed the now well-established practice by which the heir to the throne, not getting on well with his father, would make friends with the leading politicians in the Opposition. Fox was the prince's friend. Fox stood up in the House of Commons and told the members that the rumour of the prince's marriage to Mrs. FitzHerbert was a low falsehood. This he did on the assurance of the prince, as a man of honour, that he was not married or to be married to Mrs. FitzHerbert. Then, to Mrs. FitzHerbert the prince gave equally honourable assurances that he knew nothing of what Fox had said about him in the House. The gay young Prince Charming of 1780 had become not only a roué but a liar and utterly untrustworthy.

Meanwhile the debts mounted. The prince in one respect had been not ill-educated; he was the first sovereign of his line to have any interest in the arts. He loved fine paintings and fine furniture. However much he was in debt he continued to buy these beautiful things.

Still, nemesis had to be met sooner or later. In the prince's case this meant a marriage with a foreign princess. None of the early sovereigns (and few of the later ones) would think of a marriage with other than royalty, hence the absorption with German princesses, they being among the few Protestant princesses. The king, George III, ignored any marriage which his son had contracted with a commoner, secure in the knowledge that such a marriage, however much a sop to the lady's feelings, was not legal. He proceeded to prepare a list of suitable women for the prince to consider, or, more probably, for himself to consider. For the prince his attitude was summed up in the words that 'one damned German frau was as good as another.' The marriage articles were drawn for an alliance between George, Prince of Wales, heir to the crown of Great Britain and the territories belonging thereto, and Princess Caroline Amelia of Brunswick-Wolfenbuttel.

The princess was coarse and dirty in her habits. She had none of the taste which never deserted the prince; even when he was fat and old, debauched and coarse-mouthed, he could still be the patron of the arts. His new wife was to share none of his likes, and the union between them was to be one of convenience in the strictest sense of the word. He needed money to settle his debts and to enable him to live on in extravagance. He had to provide the country with an heir. He could not do the latter without a wife who met with his father's approval. He could not get the former unless he married, when Parliament would vote him certain sums to clear his difficulties. So the bargain was struck. The prince was drunk when he met his future princess, and drunk on the wedding night. However, the prince fulfilled his side of the contract by giving his wife a child, the princess Charlotte. This done, the prince ceased to live with the princess. The princess inquired whether, if Princess Charlotte died, he would wish to renew his acquaintance with her. The prince replied in terms which showed his exquisite breeding and manners. In the event of his daughter dying he would not "infringe the terms of the restriction by proposing, at any period, a connection of a more particular nature".

The prince hoped that, having done his duty, he would be allowed to escape from the bargain he had contracted. True, he did succeed in returning to Mrs. FitzHerbert for a time and in staying away from his princess. What he did not realize was the effect his attitude would have on the future queen. The princess went abroad and lived in a scandalous manner, though certainly George IV was not in a good position to criticise her conduct. When he became king she returned to England, and at the coronation she tried to make her way into the Abbey, only to find her passage barred at the king's orders. He intended to seek a divorce from his queen and only her death prevented him from proceeding with his plans.

Thus in 1820 George IV came to the throne. The tenure of the first of the two Princes of Wales in the nineteenth century had ended. He had no legitimate son, but it may be noticed in passing that he treated his daughter in the same way as all the Hanoverians treated their heirs. Her childhood was dull and dreary and no love was lost between father and daughter. However, her premature death removed her from the succession, and there was a competition among the king's elderly brothers as to who should produce the heir to the throne. Eventually a princess, Victoria, was born to the Duke and Duchess of Kent on 24th May 1819.

At the accession of George IV, his heir was his brother (afterwards William IV); and following the death of the Duke of Kent, Victoria's father, she became heir to the crown. Within eighteen years the brothers were dead, and Victoria became queen in 1837. A cleaner, brighter epoch opened in the history of British royalty. Debauchery would be no more, and the throne would become, in the final result, the guiding star of the people, for purity and decency. In the relations between sovereign and heir, however, there would still be room for much desirable change.

CHAPTER XI

Sixty Years Prince of Wales

SIXTY years: except for a few months, this was the period during which Prince Albert Edward was Prince of Wales. It was the longest tenure of the office of Prince of Wales. True, the Prince Regent, George IV, Edward's great uncle, was Prince of Wales from 1762 to 1820 but this period was not wholly given over to merely waiting for the throne. From 1812 onwards the regent made the Speech from the Throne, and was to some extent king.

Edward was born on 9th November 1841. He was created Prince of Wales on 8th December 1841. He succeeded to the throne on 22nd January 1901. The reign of 63 years of Queen Victoria, the longest in English history, had outlasted the memories of the courtiers, so that the Court of Claims when it sat at the beginning of King Edward VII's reign had many serious problems to consider. There was no one who could come forward to establish the precedents from the previous coronation.

This great interval between reigns was symbolised by the term, the Victorian era. To us, looking back over a very troubled sixty years, it seems to have been an age of calm and unbroken prosperity. The queen was firmly seated on her throne; her claims upon her people were never questioned, and the country continued to make progress without apparent effort.

The picture is far different as regards the royal family. It is true that Britain made immense progress. The nineteenth century was one of awakening of the human spirit towards its environment. At last the patient scientific researches of the centuries from the Italian Renaissance bore full fruit; from the horse-drawn carriages of the reign of George III, the world passed to the era of railways; steamships and the telegraph brought the world into closer relationship. In every sphere of life the world took on a more comfortable aspect, and there were plenty of prophets who foretold the coming of an age of plenty for every man and woman. All the great changes which mark the twentieth century were foreshadowed in the nineteenth century.

The twentieth century has witnessed an enormous change in the life of the ordinary man or woman. These changes were correctly foreseen in the nineteenth century. Unfortunately no one, or very few, foresaw the terrible risks which scientific progress could bring with it. Writers such as Winwood Reade, author of *The Martyrdom of Man*, looked forward to an age in which mankind would be dedicated to progress, an age of human perfectibility. Religion would play no part in this age, but then religion would no longer be required, for morals would have become so much an essential part of the human make-up that man would not again revert to barbaric practices. Reade (he wrote about 1875) reckoned that war would take time to eradicate but go it would—even from Europe. He did not conceive that mankind would run the risk of slipping back into a dark age. We now have witnessed the truth of this danger. The century of the Common Man is the century in which medieval cruelties have not only been revived but surpassed, and in which the subjugation of the mind as well as the torture of the body has been brought to a fine art.

None the less, the Victorians could not anticipate this, and they were right, and so are we, in regarding their age as one of immense material progress. This was true of the world in general, but especially true of Britain. The Industrial Revolution had given Britain a mighty start in the race for material prosperity. That lead would not be lost until the very end of the nineteenth century, and even then could be recovered given peace and proper application of science.

Then, in another sense, the Victorian era was one of sustained advance. It mattered very little which government was in office at Westminster. The integrity and advancement of the queen's dominions was a matter of pride to both—Gladstone and Disraeli. When Egypt threatened Britain's interests in 1882 it was Gladstone who took prompt action. Liberal or Conservative made little difference to the attitude of the rulers towards the extension of the dominions of the Great Queen. Millions of coloured people were brought under her sceptre, and to them she became much more a figure of majesty than to her own people. The great queen who ruled from afar and who dwelt in the seclusion of a castle appealed to the imaginations of the oriental and African chiefs. They were familiar from childhood with stories, often real enough, of sovereigns who lived in close seclusion, but whose word was law, and whom to see might be highly dangerous but who knew and watched over their subjects from afar.

Thus the very condition of being The Widow of Windsor, which provoked such dislike from the people in Britain, was a factor of importance in the growing empire. Steadily that empire grew until it covered one quarter of the earth's surface.

The monarchy had to adapt itself to this great change. In a sense it did, and we seldom think of Queen Victoria as one of the House of Hanover. In many history books current at the beginning of this century the queen is shown as of the House of Guelph, while Edward VII appears as first of the House of Saxe-Coburg Gotha. No one disliked this suggestion more than King Edward. He had a sure knowledge of what became an English king, including the designation of the royal house. He knew that even if he had wanted to he should not take his dynastic title from his father's family. That there have been difficulties over the true surname is shown by the problems which arose when George V in 1917 asked the Garter King of Arms for the royal surname before adopting that of Windsor.

Queen Victoria was brought up simply, without pretension, and in an excellent atmosphere. Her education was not outstandingly brilliant but adequate. She had good common sense, the will to do good, and the will to manage without her mother. From the first the new queen worked with her ministers without interference. Her political education owed much to the wisdom of such able ministers as Lord John Russell and Lord Melbourne.

Then came her marriage to a man of high moral principle, and of intellectual powers, the Prince Albert of Saxe-Coburg and Gotha. The Prince Consort, as he eventually became, took a considerable part in the direction of government. During at least one crisis, that of the American Civil War, his intervention led to a change in policy which had unforeseen results. The U.S.A. was able to go its way without fear of war with Britain. If Britain had intervened in the struggle between North and South, the South would probably have won, and the future of the U.S.A. would have been not the powerful nation as it is today but certainly two weaker nations, probably more than two, as new western states came into being. In the judgment of many continental thinkers, and particularly of the Germans, the opportunity to destroy the growing power of the U.S.A. was lost, and lost through the agency of the Prince Consort.

A man of such force of character was likely to have an impact on his family. The queen adored him, and his least word was law. He drew up a code of education for his eldest son. The boy was to become a scholar. Whether his nature would prove that of a scholar was of no moment, scholar he must become. In fact he did not. The result was that having left the schoolroom, the eldest son decided never to undergo any more academic education unless forced.

The scheme of the prince's education was drawn up by the Prince Consort after the queen and he had had the most urgent discussions about their duty towards their eldest son. They were dominated in this matter by the queen's very real fear of her uncles' example. Queen Victoria knew that only a mere generation stood between Edward, Prince of Wales and the wicked uncles. They were referred to in these terms, and it was unthinkable that the heir of the new generation should resemble them in any way. Naturally the Prince Consort's idea of a learned academic education was readily agreed to by the queen, and "poor little Wales", as *Punch* called him, was fairly launched on his ordeal.

Albert wanted his son to be like himself only more so; the queen wanted him to reproduce the qualities of her adored husband. The prince wanted to be himself. His character was one in which there were many elements of good but which could be diverted into the wrong channels. He loved pleasure, and the fault of his education was that he was never allowed any, so that when he finally broke over the traces he took to pleasures which it would have been better for him never to have tasted. He preferred to learn from men and women rather than from books, and in this he merely followed his nature. He loved crowds of persons attending upon him; he loved ceremonial and was exact in demanding it. Though of such high lineage, and heir to a great monarchy, he had a democratic attitude towards his people. He could be friends with them if he wished. The Kaiser's gibe about King Edward VII yachting with his grocer had this much truth in it. The king liked Sir Thomas Lipton's friendship, and if he found him worthy of his company others of more exalted birth than Sir Thomas could endure it likewise.

In 1859–1860 the strain of Edward's education was at last relieved. He was at Oxford and was managing to enjoy some of the pleasures of the university despite the iron regime to which he was dedicated. Then came the request from Canada for a royal visit. The queen would not go. There was no precedent for a sovereign of Britain to visit the empire. The empire was new, and for the first time soldiers from the empire had fought beside British troops in the Crimea, the forerunner of many a blood-cemented partnership. The Canadians wanted a royal visit, and would not be satisfied with less. To the astonishment of Edward, he was selected as the representative of Her Majesty. So off the prince went to Canada, where he enjoyed every minute of his stay.

He was the centre of attraction at every meeting. He was receiving for the first time the honour due to his rank and position. He felt himself at last a Prince of Wales. He was travelling under the title of the Duke of Renfrew, his parents being afraid that to travel under his real title would mean that he would get a swollen head and think himself more important than he really was. While he was on the North American continent he was invited to visit the U.S.A. Here, there was no nonsense about being Duke of Renfrew; the American President wrote to the queen about "the visit of the Prince of Wales".

Immediately after his return from America the prince was relegated to school-room conditions once more. This time it was Cambridge, and now rebellion began to manifest itself. He tried to be absent without leave, but this was frustrated by the vigilance of his guardians so that he was met at the railway station and conducted to Buckingham Palace. Then came a rumour that he contemplated matrimony. This caused the Prince Consort to go up to see his son and remonstrate with him. The Prince Consort was not well, the burden of well-doing had run him down at last. Conscious rectitude takes a toll and the Prince Consort was about to pay it. Edward's alleged romance is supposed to have hastened his death, but this is very doubtful. However, before he died the Prince Consort had come to realise that his son had a character of strength and force, but that he was of essentially different metal from himself. He realised, too, that Edward was popular merely on grounds of personality and charm, while he himself had hardly won a grudging recognition by years of devoted service.

The prince was present at his father's death-bed in December 1861. In the first flush of grief the queen gave way to Edward's desire to help by allowing him to reply to letters of condolence for her. Yet once the prime distraction of grief had passed, the queen allowed herself to indulge in the Hanoverian antipathy towards her successor. There have been members of the royal family who have spoken loyally of the queen's and the prince's instinctive and deep love and trust of each other. Certainly the prince never wavered in his loyalty to his mother. He respected her, he feared her cold unaltering wrath; he showed a filial duty to her. From her side no signs of affection appear to have shown themselves. Not that Queen Victoria after her bereavement showed a lack of affection for those who won her confidence. Her feelings for Disraeli were of warm admiration, and that great statesman understood very well the queen's need for an obvious devotion. Others of her Prime Ministers, like Gladstone, failed to kindle any feelings in her through their failure to treat her as a human being. Then there was the queen's friendship with John Brown, which led to her being lampooned in the press. She even created John Brown an

Esquire, and this rough Highland servant was allowed to take
liberties with the heir apparent, with people about the court,
and even with the queen herself. He sometimes addressed her
as "woman" and indeed he seemed to have forgotten her
royal rank altogether. The whole situation was ridiculous, but
the queen refused to budge from her preference for John Brown.
His name made its appearance in the Court Circular, including
references to his relations as late as 1895.

The one person to whom the queen would not turn for
support or for comfort was the Prince of Wales. She professed
to regard him as responsible for the death of her "angel"
as she termed the Prince Consort. It followed as a natural
consequence of this dislike of the prince that he was not
allowed any state office or function. He was far more versed
in the world and its rulers than she was but he was treated by
the queen he was to succeed as though he were a child. After
his father's death his education was to go on on the same lines
as laid down by the Prince Consort. How long this tiresome
martyrdom would have been stretched no one knows; the
queen and the Prince Consort (in his case there was some
slight change of view just before his death) viewed their eldest
with the same essential hostility so marked through earlier
Hanoverian reigns. As the prince's charm won thousands of
admirers and friends, as he conquered fresh realms, such as
among "the immoral French", he gained ever less esteem
from his mother.

In 1862 the prince escaped from his prison. He married.
Like the Prince Regent, his marriage was his salvation but for
very different reasons, just as the very beautiful lady who became Princess of Wales was very different from the unfortunate
Caroline. He married Alexandra of Denmark. The English
people did not wholeheartedly share their queen's love for
everything German.

They welcomed with joy the beautiful Dane, and to Edward
she proved always a true and loyal helpmate, while he gave
to his partner a respect and courtesy which many of her
predecessors would have envied.

'Le Roi s'amuse' had been a motto of many kings; Prince
Edward loved amusement. He hated boredom. He liked

attractive women. They liked him. His position gave him unrivalled opportunities of meeting women of beauty and talent. He had a large number of lady friends—like Lily Langtry, the Jersey Lily, and the Countess of Warwick, who only bored him when she tried to make a Socialist of him. Sir Sidney Lee, who wrote his official life, could hardly be expected to deal with that side of the monarch's life. He was too near the time when the king had lived.

Modern biographers are not so cautious, and yet even so very little is really known about King or Prince Edward's affairs of the heart.

He loved London and its pleasures. More still, he loved Paris, which he visited so much that it became his second city. He travelled extensively in Europe. He knew the royal houses of Europe as well as any man can know his relations. He knew all that should be known of ceremonial matters, particularly uniforms. He cared for state. He cared to some extent for lack of state, but woe betide any who presumed to impose upon the seemingly democratic side of his nature. To call him by a nickname was to ensure the end of his friendship. To touch him was to feel the full extent of royal displeasure. Yet friendship was a real thing to him. Unlike some other kings, he stood by his friends.

In his taste for pleasure and search for it, inevitably there were awkward moments. There was the Mordaunt divorce case when the Prince of Wales went into the witness-box, and after a series of questions about his knowledge of Lady Mordaunt he was asked: "Has there ever been any improper familiarity or criminal connection of any sort between yourself and Lady Mordaunt?" "There has not," was the prince's answer. Still, it must be agreed that it was a remarkable thing for the heir to the throne to be a witness in a divorce action. Public opinion was not too happy about the matter, though both Queen Victoria and Princess Alexandra showed their loyalty to Edward very clearly. This was in 1869. It was more than twenty years later that the other court case in which he featured came up, long after his part in the Mordaunt case had been forgotten.

This was in 1890 when Sir William Gordon-Cumming

brought an action for slander against some society men who alleged that he had cheated at baccarat. The Prince of Wales was called as a witness—and the fact that his name was mixed up in the case was ill received by the public.

The newspapers of the Victorian period had very few of the inhibitions which exist in Fleet Street today. There were then continual lampoons about the widow of Windsor and John Brown. There were suggestions, and very pointed ones, in cartoons about Queen Victoria retiring—going out of business was the term—while the young prince and princess mounted the throne. There were many pointed allusions to Edward's resemblance to his maternal rather than his paternal ancestors. One of them must have caused much merriment. In it Edward was shown as Hamlet following his father's ghost, who bore a strong resemblance to the old Prince Regent, while Edward exclaimed, "I'll follow thee." Tranby Croft (home of one Arthur Wilson, where the Gordon-Cumming affair had taken place) was sketched in another lampoon.

We may sum up by saying that in Edward at this period we have a man of great ability, a lover of pleasure, far from sharing his father's liking for study and books and serious amusement, but also a man born to govern, with a natural bent for knowledge of affairs of state. It was at this stage that the worst defect in Edward's nature was allowed to widen and develop. Had he been from an early period required to attend to affairs of state he would still have found time for his pleasures but not for so many of them. He would have been willing to act as Viceroy of Ireland, a position which several statesmen of the reign wished him to occupy, but his mother was adamant. He could not go. Had he gone, he might have commended himself to the Irish, to have better appreciated their point of view and to have alleviated their conditions. The Irish question might not have developed into the ugly thing it was to become.

Until he was fifty the prince was treated by Victoria as though he were still a small boy in a schoolroom. He was not to know of matters of state. "I know as much about what is going on as I can find from the newspapers," he complained. Eventually, by the help of the more far-seeing statesmen, he was enabled to know something of the affairs of the state over which he was to rule. Before that time, he knew as much as he could glean from conversation, and his experience of government was limited to sitting on committees.

Prince Edward found one matter of immense difficulty as he grew older. His nephew, the German Emperor, was his mother's favourite but not Edward's. The man was impossible by the prince's standards. He tried to disparage his uncle by dwelling on his rank as a crowned head. Edward of course was the representative of the greatest sovereign in the world, and heir to her monarchy, but the Kaiser, backed very often by Queen Victoria, wished to take first place. He had many disadvantages as compared with the prince. One, physical, was his withered arm, the other his preoccupation with uniforms —he could not look kingly in plain clothes. Edward was the leader of fashion in Europe. What he decreed by his example was followed by Europe—by men of any pretension to fashion. The Kaiser was hopelessly outdistanced here. Even in the sphere of protocol and uniform no greater master existed than the prince. He liked everything to be properly arranged. When he became king he gave his Prime Minister a ceremonial place. Hitherto the First Minister of the Crown had been a person unknown to Precedence. The Order of Merit was another recognition of the new need to reward men of outstanding qualities who were not of military, naval or political professions.

The hostility of uncle and nephew had sad consequences. If they had been able to get on together the peace of Europe might have been kept. There are those who say that the Kaiser had two natures: one, theatrical and arrogant for public use; the other, more tolerant and sensible, for his intimates. According to those who hold this view the Kaiser was saddened beyond measure by the approach of hostilities in 1914.

If so, he contrived to keep his feelings hidden and did not allow them to influence events. The Kaiser earned the detestation of the English people, though after 1933 when a schizophrenic housepainter came to rule Germany (by a vote, by the way), the Kaiser seemed, by comparison, a gentleman. Indeed one hardly thinks he would have had his political opponents murdered in a concentration camp.

So the very long apprenticeship of the Prince of Wales passed, and in 1901 he came to the long-awaited throne. He came with a maturity of experience and of the world which few of his predecessors could have matched. He came with a formal education which had left little influence upon him. He came, too, with a friendly relationship with his heir which was seen for the first time in the House of Hanover.

CHAPTER XII

Princes of the Twentieth Century — I

THERE have been three Princes of Wales created in the twentieth century: Prince George, afterwards George V; the present Duke of Windsor, and H.R.H. the present Prince of Wales, whose creation dates from July 1958.

There are some considerable contrasts and differences in the preparation of each of these for his task. Prince George had the disability that he was not the elder son of his father. The latter was Prince Albert Victor Christian Edward, known as Prince Eddie, later the Duke of Clarence. It was a curiosity of Queen Victoria's reign that all her male grandchildren should bear the name of the Prince Consort, Albert. She fondly expected that Edward VII would be known as Albert I, and that his son in turn would be Albert II. In this, as in so many other things, Edward VII showed how well he understood the feelings of his people, who appreciated, as apparently Queen Victoria did not, that Edward was a native name with a ring of age-old historical associations about it.

Prince Eddie was never Prince of Wales, for he died nine years before his father succeeded to the throne. In the education of the princes Canon Dalton (father of Dr. Hugh Dalton) had a considerable part. It was largely at his suggestion that when Prince George was to enter the Navy Prince Eddie also entered the service. They cruised in the *Bacchante* for three years, though, during the cruise, the well-known Hanoverian aversion to the heir being exposed to warfare manifested itself. Off South Africa the ship was ordered to Cape Town because the Boers, making ready for their later struggle, were in revolt against British authority. The queen intervened at once. Neither boy must be near any fighting.

On leaving the *Bacchante* the princes went to Switzerland with Dalton to study languages, at which the future George V was never very good. Then their careers parted. The younger prince was to be a naval officer. The elder had to have a broader education, befitting one who would eventually come to the throne. Their pre-naval training had been secluded from other boys, just as their father's and their other Hanoverian forebears had been. However, there was one advance in Prince Eddie's education at the university, for, unlike Edward VII, he was not kept out of Cambridge itself, although the privileges which he was granted made his position so painfully different from that of other undergraduates that he could not properly participate in Cambridge life.

The Prince of Wales showed his ideas about the education of his heir by taking Prince Eddie about with him to functions where he could learn the manner in which royalty were expected to behave. Unfortunately the prince soon tired of these formal occasions and he found it difficult to simulate interest. However, the subject of his marriage was soon broached and without much trouble, for the Duke of Clarence was a docile and obedient son who did what was expected of him without demur—he was engaged to his cousin Princess May of Teck, like him a descendant of George III.

Only a few weeks after the engagement the prince's life had ended. He had never been strong and he succumbed to influenza and pneumonia. Prince George now stood in the succession to the throne, and he knew that in a few years he would be Prince of Wales. It meant, as he regretfully realised, that his naval career was over. He would in due course be Admiral of the Fleet, but this rank would not have come, as he had hoped, from following his chosen profession but as a necessary consequence of his being king.

The question of Prince George's marriage now assumed priority. He was the Prince of Wales's remaining son and the queen was insistent on his marrying. He did not welcome marriage with a German princess, and in view of the developments twenty years later, it was as well that he did not. H had known his cousin the Princess May from childhood, and it was not unnatural that they should console each other after the Duke of Clarence's death in 1892. Soon they became deeply attached to each other and what was to prove a very happy marriage was quietly arranged. The future king was to differ in this respect from many of his German predecessors in that he had married the woman of his choice.

The nation benefited from the change of the heirs to the throne, for the Duke of Clarence could hardly have been called a strong character; and Prince George had seen much more of the work-a-day world than had most of the preceding kings for two hundred years. He became Duke of York and settled down to learn the duties of a constitutional sovereign, as far as they can be learned from books and conversation and without participation in public affairs. As the Prince of Wales had been barred from such participation, it is obvious that his son was.

At last the old queen died, and Edward VII ascended the throne. His heir was a man of thirty-six and he was quickly sent on a tour of the empire during which he was to open the new Federal Parliament of Australia. It was not until his return in 1901 that he was created Prince of Wales. Then he found how much his father had learned from the prohibition of his own education. The king ordered that state documents which were sent to him should be shown to the prince. For the first time in the history of the Hanoverian dynasty a reigning sovereign was on good terms with his heir. Father and son might not always see eye to eye, that would be exceptional between any father and son, but generally their relationship was one of mutual confidence.

The value of the confidence which had existed between King Edward and his son showed itself when shortly after George V's accession in 1910 a constitutional crisis arose, the first for a century. It was a serious ordeal for a new king to find his countrymen acutely divided over the centuries-old disputes between Commons and Lords. These discords had assumed new proportions from the growth of democratic feeling and the fiery eloquence of Lloyd George.

The new Prince of Wales was Edward, eldest son of George V and heir to the world's mightiest empire. So we are where we began with the old walls of the Welsh stronghold witnessing a pageantry they had been denied for centuries. No Prince of Wales between the first (and his presentation to the Welsh people is legendary) and the twentieth had been shown to the Welsh in Wales and at Caernarvon. Ludlow was usually the place where the princes went to be near their Welsh dominions, though their investitures took place in London or at a royal palace in England.

Yet not quite the end; for twenty-five years the Prince of Wales of 1911 was to fascinate the people he was meant to govern. No prince in our history has had such a popularity among the ordinary folk of the land as Edward, Prince of Wales. During the First World War he desperately longed for the opportunity to prove himself a soldier, as had one after another of the Hanoverian Princes of Wales. Like them, the prince was denied his heart's desire.

Care for the ex-servicemen whose war he had shared was to be one of the abiding preoccupations of the Prince of Wales; another was to be his great interest in the unemployed. In his memoirs the Duke of Windsor lets us see some of the sadness which he could not help feeling about the grim canker of unemployment.

The Prince of Wales toured the vast empire as none had before him. He travelled thousands of miles and was hailed by millions of spectators. He was an ambassador of empire—not only in the empire, but outside, in vast areas like Latin America, where his efforts earned the approbation of the Prime Minister, Stanley Baldwin, who later had the misfortune to be the instrument of his abdication.

What was the training of the Prince of Wales for his task? He was the son of the first Hanoverian heir to the throne to be at ease and happy with his father and sovereign. Did King George V learn from his own experience? Only, it has to be admitted, to a limited degree. He was a family man who loved his children, but he was not in advance of his age. He listened carefully to the reasons advanced, by tutors and advisers, that the Prince of Wales and the future Duke of York should go to school with other boys. He listened but did not agree; he felt that the system under which he and the

Duke of Clarence had been educated was the best—namely, a private schoolroom and then the Navy.

So the Prince of Wales had the restricted education of the tutor's room, and then the levelling experience of the Navy. The Duke of Windsor has told us much of his life in the early stages, so that it contains no secrets. The Navy was followed by a short stay at Oxford, then language study, and after that the Army. As it happened, the Army proved to be a wider experience than had been anticipated, for try how the authorities might they could not altogether keep the Prince of Wales at headquarters.

It has often been suggested that the Duke of Windsor in many respects bore a greater resemblance to Edward VII than to George V; that the solid qualities of his father had somehow been overlaid. This criticism overlooks many strong resemblances between George V and Edward VIII, and equally deep differences between Edward VII and Edward VIII. For one thing, and this very important, the Duke of Windsor, as he says himself of the Caernarvon investiture, had no liking for ceremonies in which honours were paid to him. Edward VII revelled in stately ceremonial, in which the king, or future king, must be the centre. Edward VII had a great knowledge of uniforms, decorations, ceremonies, and, of course, of the ramifications and pedigree of European royalty. In this respect Edward VIII never approached his grandfather. On the other hand, his grandson knew infinitely more of the conditions of life of the poor and unemployed, not only than any other member of the royal family but than the cabinet as well. During years of patient labour he gained this insight by going all over the land to visit ex-servicemen and unemployed men's clubs.

Then again, however much "Guelpho the Gay" (Edward VII) loved pleasure he would never have thought of renouncing his throne. One does not choose to be a prince any more than to be a pauper, but to Edward VII the fact that he was so born was a responsibility of which he kept others reminded as well as himself.

When the Prince of Wales in due course became Edward VIII he reached the throne with a popularity granted to very few kings or queens in our history. Yet, within a year his reign had ended with his abdication. This can only be described as a tragedy.

That the monarchy took this hard blow, unknown for almost 250 years, is a tribute to the hold which it possessed on the British people. The most popular figure of Britain's royalty gave up the headship of the vast empire, and George VI by the Grace of God succeeded Edward VIII by the Grace of God. The cynical might say that one functionary had gone and another taken his place. The power of the premier had been demonstrated. Although outwardly there was no sign of a fundamental change, yet 1936 marks very definitely a stage in the evolution of the British monarchy.

Lord Bryce, the author of the famous work, *The Holy Roman Empire*, thought that even in the 20th century a sovereign of ability and character could have put a strong personal stamp upon British affairs; could have regained for the throne some power. Any possibility of such happening has been destroyed by the abdication of 1936. It has been made clear that a sovereign must accept the advice of the Prime Minister, or if that advice is not accepted, then it is the sovereign and not the minister who must resign. There is always another potential sovereign who can be put forward to fill the royal place. All power, except in affairs of private life, has left the British Crown. Nothing written now approaches the appalling tone of Charles Bradlaugh's *The Impeachment of the House of Brunswick*, a work first published in 1871. Nine editions appeared in the author's lifetime, and the tenth in 1892 brought out by his daughter. Bradlaugh was a British M. P. That his book should have been published in England in the later part of Victoria's reign is a proof of the continuance of a small amount of antiroyalist feeling in a certain circle. He did not hesitate to include in his book a statement that George III was, before his accession, married to Hannah Lightfoot, in Curzon Street Chapel, Mayfair, London. "Great doubt has, however, been cast on the fact as well as the legality of the marriage. It would if in all respects valid, have rendered null, as a bigamous contract, the subsequent marriage entered into by the King. Dr. Doran alleges that the Prince of Wales, afterwards George IV, when needing money in later years, used this Lightfoot marriage as a threat against his royal parents—that is, he threatened to expose his mother's shame and his own illegitimacy if the Queen would not use her influence with Pitt. Glorious family, these Brunswicks!" (*op. cit.* page 42–3). Later (page 50) the author says that Hannah died in 1764 leaving children by George III, of whom nothing is known. When he reached the reign of Queen Victoria, Bradlaugh's remarks were mild in comparison with his earlier utterances, but even so it is remarkable that they should have been published at that time.

Certainly nothing resembling Bradlaugh's diatribes is now published, but on the other hand the monarchy is frequently put under the microscope of opinion expressed by well-known publicists and so-called experts. Many of these people are not aware of the full facts relating to monarchy in Britain. They are not cognizant of the philosophy which attends monarchy. By this I do not mean any puzzling mystique which defies rational analysis but refer to the fact that from the emergence of the English monarchy 1100 years ago, there has been only one break in its continuity, and that for only 11 years. Such a persistence of an institution would seem to indicate that it is agreeable to the outlook of the nation. Most of the critics are probably incapable of understanding tradition, national or otherwise, but even the dimmest of intellectuals could perhaps grasp that a drastic change in a nation's oldest institution—for monarchy in Britain goes back in its origins to the earliest English settlement—might well throw that country on to a strange and disastrous course.

These considerations are apposite as we consider the life of the third Prince of Wales in this century. Prince Charles cannot be thought of without the subject of his succession to the throne. On an actuarial basis we can calculate that there will not be a succession until the 21st century, barring a fatality, the premature death of Elizabeth II. Thus the prince faces the probability of a 40 year tenure of his position as Prince of Wales. Since this must have been in the minds of his parents, the nature of his education must have been related to peculiar circumstances of his future life and to the unprecedented nature of British external affairs.

Ever since the reign of William the Conqueror (1066–87), the rulers of England have always possessed territories outside England. For the great part of 900 years, England, which could be said in the 11th century to have been colonized by Normandy, has been a colonizing power. A not implausible thesis can be made to show that colonizing has been a feature of English life from the very beginning, in the 5th to 6th centuries.

Now this process is coming to an end. The British Empire is gone; the few poor relics of it will soon receive a penury laden independence or be handed over to foreign powers against the wishes of the inhabitants. In the British Isles, separatist movements are growing, with the object of an independent Scotland or Wales, a clamour rises from the Irish Republic for union with Northern Ireland (part of the United Kingdom) and the Isle of Man and the Channel Islands talk of imitating the Unilateral Declaration of Independence in Southern Rhodesia. On the face of things, one would say that there is the prospect of a return to the arrangements of the Heptarchy, before there was a royal realm of all England, without the remote conception of a united Britain.

Along with the collapse of the British colonial system, goes the breakdown in the national institutions. The House of Lords faces a drastic reconstitution, and has already changed so much that it has scarcely more than its name in common with the House as it was half a century back. The established Church of England has lost adherence of most of the people. In a desperate bid for further support a scheme was put forward for union with the Methodists. The House of Commons has lost its character as representative of the people and consists of party nominees doing as they are told by the party bosses. The masses of legislation pushed through by these docile M.P.s cannot be learned or digested even by the legal profession; in the latest volume of *Halsbury's Statutes,* for 1968, there are included no less than 68 new Acts of Parliament, running to 2200 pages. Can it be wondered that the members of the general public do not even know how they break the law, until they are charged with a breach of an obscure section of an Act or of some regulation made by a minister of the Crown?

In this rapidly deteriorating condition, with Britain's other institutions running down, can the monarchy escape? Will there be a King Charles III? Since the facts set out above cannot escape the attention of intelligent observers, and this includes the royal family, the upbringing of Prince Charles has clearly been conducted in order to cope with the challenge of the future.

CHAPTER XIII

Princes of the Twentieth Century — II

H.R.H. the present Prince of Wales was born on 14th November 1948, christened Charles Philip Arthur George on 15th December of that year. By Letters Patent approved by King George VI on 22nd October 1948 he was to 'have and at all times enjoy the style, title or attribute of Royal Highness and the titular dignity of Prince.' On the accession of Princess Elizabeth as Her Majesty Queen Elizabeth II, H.R.H. Prince Charles became Duke of Cornwall, in accordance with the charter of Edward III of 1337.

The title of Prince of Wales is conferred upon the eldest son of the reigning sovereign when it pleases the sovereign to do so. It was therefore a matter of considerable interest as to the time when Her Majesty would create the Duke of Cornwall Prince of Wales. The occasion was felicitously chosen, when on 26th July 1958, at the Empire Commonwealth Games at Cardiff, the announcement was made that 'The Queen has been pleased to order Letters Patent to be passed under the Great Seal for creating His Royal Highness Prince Charles Philip Arthur George, Duke of Cornwall and Rothesay, Earl of Carrick, Baron of Renfrew, Lord of the Isles and Great Steward of Scotland, Prince of Wales and Earl of Chester.'

The creation as Prince of Wales was not to be followed by his investiture until 1st July 1969. At the announcement of the creation at the Games in Cardiff there was very great enthusiasm, but in the intervening 11 years there grew up the separatist movements mentioned at the close of the last chapter. Fortunately the investiture and the prince's subsequent tour through Wales passed off with hardly an untoward incident and indeed with very great enthusiasm on the part of most Welsh people.

Previously there had been some use of bombs mainly in Cardiff, but it is to be hoped that the prince's pleasing personality and his obvious liking for Wales will more and more endear him to the people of the principality. When this book was first published in 1959, I was able to include only four pages about Prince Charles, who was then only 11. With the advantage of another decade to draw upon, I shall still avail myself of some of the material I then used because I think it has a relevance given to it by the subsequent developments. For the convenience of readers when passages from the 1959 edition are used they are shown between inverted commas. Sir Richard Colville, whose great kindness I have acknowledged, lent to me several books on the royal family, the facts in which had all been checked by Her Majesty. This gives an enhanced interest to the material in quotes.

I think that the prince's first 20 years should be considered under three heads: (1) his family circle; (2) his education, and (3) his position now and for the future as Prince of Wales.

The prince was nearly two years old when on 15th August 1950, Princess Anne (Elizabeth Alice Louise) was born at Clarence House. The two other children of the queen and Prince Philip are much younger. Prince Andrew (Albert Christian Edward) was born at Buckingham Palace on 19th February 1960, and Prince Edward (Antony Richard Louis) on 10th March 1964. The gap in age between the two sections of the family has meant that the elder children have naturally been much together and are in any case great friends. Together they have travelled, as children and as adults.

"His voyage, with Princess Anne, to Malta in 1954 was the first stage of his journey to meet the queen and Prince Philip returning from their Commonwealth tour. From pictures and films taken at the time it is clear that the prince and his sister enjoyed every minute of it. They were impressed, as every child would be by the great white fortress walls of Valetta and the splendid ships lying at anchor in the harbour." There are delightful photographs which show the prince and princess with two blue jackets of the Royal Navy in the resourceful manner of seamen pointing out the sights of Gibraltar.

"After a brief stay they went on to Tobruk in Africa, where

they met the queen and Prince Philip, then voyaged home with them, visiting Malta again and Gibraltar en route. At Gibraltar the royal children, like many other visitors, were delighted to feed the apes which live on the rock.

"In 1956 Prince Charles and Princess Anne again sailed on the Royal Yacht *Britannia*, this time from Southampton to the Western Isles of Scotland. Off South Uist and Benbecula Princess Anne celebrated her sixth birthday, and she and her brother watched her birthday mail being delivered by helicopter to a destroyer and then transferred by line to the *Britannia*. During this voyage the prince and princess had their first experience of a severe storm which necessitated the *Britannia* shifting from exposed waters to the South of Kerrera, where the queen and Prince Philip eventually rejoined her."

In 1967 at the Opening of Parliament when the queen read the Speech from the Throne, Prince Charles as heir to the throne sat on the queen's right and Princess Anne on her left. This was the first time that they had been present officially at this important regal ceremonial. Again, after the exacting ordeal of the investiture, Charles and Anne went on a holiday to Malta. No one, however, who has seen the photographs of Charles with his little brothers, can doubt that he is warmly affectionate to them, too, as indeed in all his family circle.

Between father and son there is a sound friendship, perhaps as often happens the greater because they differ so much. The Duke of Edinburgh is a forceful character who could have made a substantial mark in life had he been born to a private station. His forthright speeches show how chafed he feels at times in his official position. The effect which his remarks have upon the left-wing politicians demonstrates the soundness of his outlook. To be the son of such a father must then be an exacting inheritance, and but for mutual understanding and regard could be an incubus. It is a tribute to the queen and her husband's upbringing of Prince Charles that he should have developed into the intelligent and essentially happy young man that he is.

From very early days the queen has been particularly studious of her eldest son's education. She has listened carefully to the views of experts, but probably the greatest influence on Prince Charles's scholastic course has been Prince Philip. One of the great objects of the royal parents has been to endeavour that Prince Charles should be brought up as far as possible like other boys.

As far as possible. But, of course, he can never be wholly like other lads of his age and time. "Yet nothing could make clearer to the young prince the difference, however great the effort to prevent it, between himself and other boys than the visit to Malta in 1954—when he was six. He sailed in the Royal Yacht *Britannia*. He was escorted to Portsmouth by his grandmother, Queen Elizabeth the Queen Mother, and by Princess Margaret. There was a special train; the prince shook hands with the R.N. captain, Capt. J.S. Dalglish, who was at that time in command of the Royal Yacht.

"Even before this Prince Charles had witnessed part of the impressive ceremony of the coronation. From a privileged place in Westminster Abbey he was present at the actual moment when the queen, his mother, was crowned. It was said of Queen Victoria that she was not told about her royal future, but was allowed to discover it for herself from her lessons in history. How very different the circumstance of the present heir to the throne. The prince has seen his mother the centre of a nation's ceremonies. The home in which he lives and the style of progress which he makes in company with his parents cannot but make the young prince aware of the difference between himself and other boys."

Yet the Prince of Wales enjoys one enormous advantage over all his predecessors. None of them had ever attended a school. In medieval times this had mattered little, for there were compensating factors. Very early in life the heir to the throne was initiated into the arts of war, diplomacy, and government. Formal education in the scholastic sense was probably crammed into the medieval prince's early years by tutors and supplemented later in intervals between practical initiation in the tasks of kingship. In later times under the Tudors and Stuarts, book learning was seriously inculcated by private tutors, often with extreme severity. In the Hanoverian period when the sons of the nobility and well-to-do were normally sent to boarding school, generations passed without a Prince of Wales being allowed to enjoy the companionship of other boys of the same age. George III's education could very well have been improved by his presence in a school with other boys. As for Edward VII he was never allowed to be free of the narrowing tutelage of private pedagogues and even his participation in university life was completely distorted and ruined.

Very different has been the education of Prince Charles. In his beginnings he was taught at home by governesses and for a short time by a tutor, before he went at the beginning of 1957 to a preparatory school in London, Hill House in Hans Place, Knightsbridge where the founder and headmaster was Colonel Townend. One of the queen's greatest desires was that the boy should not be given undue publicity, not only because of the bad effect which it might have on the prince but because of the unpleasantness which it would certainly entail for his schoolfellows.

Here a matter of criticism obtrudes, in so far as Prince Charles by being sent to Hill House may be regarded as having been committed to the English public school type of education. It was argued by certain critics that he should have gone to a state school, in order that he might from the very beginning of his education share in the experiences of his future subjects. There are two powerful arguments against this course. The aim of keeping publicity away from the prince's education could not have been achieved in the very open purlieus of an English state school. The appetite for news of royalty seems insatiable in English society, at least as interpreted by the newspapers. As things were, at Prince Charles's schools special precautions had to be taken to exclude the activities of reporters and photographers. As no other pupil would be subject to such attentions it was clearly essential that the publicity agencies should be kept away.

The second argument against state schools is more controversial; simply that they do not provide the best all round education. Most public schools in England (the term by the way means the very opposite of its use in Canada and America where English public schools would be termed private schools) have long waiting lists, although fees are always being increased. The critics of these schools always complain that boys who attend them possess unfair advantages, a charge which appears to imply superiority of instruction. Finally anyone in England who has had much experience in dealing with senior boys from both ranges of school, as I have, would almost certainly give the preference to boys educated in public (i.e. really private) sectors of education.

Very interesting indeed were the results of the prince's studies at Hill House. He has never liked mathematics, is reasonably good at languages, but loves history and the arts. For organized games, he showed little enthusiasm. Apart from the formal education and the participation in sports, the prince's gains from being at Hill House were principally in mixing with other boys of his own age group of 9–10. He had no special privileges at the school and his parents would come to a sports day like any other parents.

At the end of his short period at Hill House, Prince Charles was sent to a preparatory school in Berkshire called Cheam. This was a 300-year-old school which had been taken out of London by its founder for fear of the Great Plague in 1665. It had settled at Cheam in the county of Surrey and retained its name when it was moved to Berkshire. Prince Philip is an old boy of the school and his influence led to Charles being sent to Cheam. At Hill House he had been a day boy, going down each morning in the care of a chauffeur, but every evening he would be back in the home atmosphere. Now he had to take the plunge of becoming a boarder away from home for a term at a time.

Prince Charles had a certain shyness in his early days which made his entry into the world of school a torture. This trait in his character has been apparently overcome if we may judge by his splendid bearing in the investiture and general behaviour in Wales. One can sympathize with any lad of ten suddenly finding himself away from a familiar atmosphere and surrounded by strangers. Moreover, no matter what efforts had been made to minimize his special position, nothing could alter the fact that he was different. At first his schoolmates at Cheam scarcely felt that they could be over friendly with him in view of his inevitably special position.

Gradually the shyness and aloofness wore away, aided by the ability with which a special detective who took up lodgings in a house in the grounds of Cheam, kept out any undesirable publicity hunters. His formal education progressed to the extent that he could pass the public schools entrance examination, a *sine qua non* for all who seek to enter an English public school. He progressed in appreciation of the arts. He learned to play the piano, and he sang in the school choir. He loves music, and the 'cello later became one of the musical instruments which he plays. Then, too, at Cheam he began to show that delight in theatrical performances which is characteristic of him. He played the part of Richard, Duke of Gloucester, later Richard III, in *The Last Baron*, a school play; the boy who should have taken the part had left, and Charles had the experience of acting as one of his mother's predecessors (not his or her ancestor in the direct line, only in the collateral sense).

Nothing can illustrate more clearly the difficulties inherent in the prince's position than the manner in which he learnt officially of his creation by the queen as Prince of Wales. In company with some of the other boys at Cheam, Prince Charles was allowed to watch on television the opening of the Commonwealth Games at Cardiff. As the queen was prevented by illness from being present, her place was taken by Prince Philip, and the queen gave a recorded message to the spectators. In this she announced that Prince Charles was then created Prince of Wales. He, a boy of 9 years and 8 months old, heard this in the midst of his schoolfellows and must have realized something of his destiny. At the time of his creation as Prince of Wales, he automatically became a K.G., Knight of the Garter, for the Prince of Wales must always be one of the foundation members of the Order. In former days a sovereign's eldest son was often dubbed even while he was a child, an amusing commentary on the up-to-the-minute theory that modern youth matures more quickly than in previous generations. History abounds with examples of teen-age graduates and holders of offices to which no modern youth has the remotest chance of being appointed. The prince though nominally a K.G. was not, therefore, dubbed a knight until he was of an age to take his proper part in the ceremonies of the Order. His entry into the Order took place at a Chapter held on 17th June 1968 at Windsor Castle when his mother gave him the traditional accolade of knighthood, by touching him with a drawn sword lightly on each shoulder.

From early years the prince, under the influence of his father, has learnt to be a keen follower of field sports, especially shooting and fishing. Prince Philip combines a love of shooting on the big scale with impassioned appeals for the preservation of wild life. It is again due to Prince Philip's influence that he started in his later adolescence to play polo, a game which he greatly enjoys.

The extent to which life at Cheam had cured the prince of his shyness was seen in an experience which would be remarkable for any youth of 13. In February 1962, during his father's absence, he took Prince Philip's place as host at one of the queen's informal luncheon parties at Buckingham Palace.

In 1962 the prince went to his public school—a public school with a difference. Here again he followed his father, in going to the latter's old school at Gordonstoun near Elgin, in Scotland. This school was founded in 1919 by Prince Max of Baden who appointed a Jew, Dr. Kurt Hahn, as headmaster. The latter had been compelled to leave Germany in the Hitlerite persecutions and to settle in Scotland. When Hahn retired, Mr. F.R.G. Chew became headmaster, and it was he who received Prince Philip when he brought over Prince Charles for the first day of his new experience. The essence of Gordonstoun lies perhaps in the emphasis on self-reliance, and outdoor activities apart from organized games. While the latter are, of course, played at the school, and the usual curriculum of English higher education is followed, the peculiar quality of the school is in its stress on the development of character. The head boy of Gordonstoun is called the Guardian, a term reminiscent of the class of rulers described in Plato's *Republic*, a work which was very much in Dr. Hahn's mind in the forming of his school.

Prince Philip had been supremely happy at Gordonstoun and had shone as an athlete. Prince Charles was to achieve great success in other fields. He won the Silver Medal, his father's award (under the Duke of Edinburgh's Award Scheme, which gives recognition to public service such as life saving and to physical fitness) and he reached the honoured position of Guardian. The prince's love of drama was seen in the skilled performance which he gave in the name part of *Macbeth*

The impression which one gains is of an extremely likeable
youth, considerate and kind, courteous as a prince should be
deeply interested in varied aspects of life—history, archaeology
music, out-of-doors activities, and the drama.

The prince is, of course, a member of the Church of England
as no British sovereign may occupy the throne, unless he or she
is a Protestant, and a member of the Established Church. He
was prepared for his confirmation by the Very Reverend
Robin Woods, the Dean of Windsor. To a sensitive boy this i
one of the greatest experiences of his life, one which it is difficul
to put into words; a great moment in the development of the
Christian life; in short, a spiritual experience and one which
the prince has deeply appreciated.

Gordonstoun certainly contributed greatly to the prince'
development but in 1966 came a welcome change, for it wa
decided that Prince Charles should spend six months at ar
Australian school. It was arranged that he should go to Geelong
Church of England Grammar School in Victoria; or rather to
the extension of the school at Timbertop in the Australian out
back. There was a close resemblance to Gordonstoun, and
Timbertop was modelled on the Scottish school. The pupils a
Geelong go to Timbertop for a year in their school course i
the age group 14–15. Prince Charles was thus with boys som
two years younger than himself. The opportunities for outdoo
activities, with a considerable reduction in bookwork, wer
many and varied, much more so than in Scotland. They in
cluded sheep shearing, gold panning, gem hunting, tree felling
walking long distances in the bush, and climbing peaks. From
February to July 1966, the prince lived at Timbertop (apar
from breaks between the two terms) enjoying this great change
before returning to Gordonstoun to finish off his school days.

It was during his stay in Australia that he was afforded a
experience which can only be described as spiritual. At the en
of his first term at Timbertop he went in company with othe
pupils to visit the Church of England mission stations in th
overseas territory of the Australian Commonwealth in Papu
and New Guinea. There he saw scenes which must bear
resemblance in many respects to the work of the Church i

every country which does not possess a high indigenous culture —to some extent, although the parallel is not by any means exact—to the England of the 6th century, or perhaps a better example to the Church's work in Scandinavia in the 10th to 11th centuries. In such lands the Church is called on to convert, to minister spiritually, and to give educational and medical services.

In the Cathedral at Dogura on the Sunday of his visit, Prince Charles was a communicant with nearly a thousand others, the service being in the native tongue of the converts. This was an experience that, as regards numbers, could hardly be equalled in modern England, in an Anglican Cathedral. In an essay which he wrote about his experiences in this visit, Prince Charles said: 'I would like to mention how fresh and sincere I found the Church at Dogura. Everyone was so eager to take part in the services and the singing was almost deafening. One felt that it might almost be the original Church. Where Christianity is new, it must be much easier to enter into the whole spirit of it whole heartedly, and it is rather wonderful that you can still go somewhere where this strikes you.' (Quoted in *To Be A King*, by Dermot Morrah, 1969, p. 143.)

By a paradox, the feeling of the newness of Christ's gospel came home to many who served during the last war especially in far off places. The sense of being away from all the cursed entanglements of modern civilized life, made the Gospel precepts strike home, even in the midst of warfare in a way almost impossible to capture in modern England. It is this kind of impression which the prince described.

It was during the end of his Gordonstoun time that the prince was appointed Guardian. In that last term he had his 18th birthday. From time to time he could now be summoned to act as a Counsellor of State. Probably of more importance to the prince was the fact that he had passed both his A Level Examinations, the subjects being French and History. He could look forward to going on to a university and for the first time he was of an age to be consulted on the choice.

It proved to be Trinity College, Cambridge, and the prince is at the time of this writing (late 1969) an undergraduate in residence, having gone up in October 1967. It is hoped that he will, despite all the inevitable calls on his time, go right on to the Tripos Examination and take his B.A. degree. He has already taken second class honours in the Archaeology and Anthropology Tripos, Part I. His acting ability has found full vent at Cambridge in the amateur dramatic societies. As a singing dustman in an undergraduate revue he gained world-wide publicity. He has picked up a knowledge of Greek during his Australian schooling, for, by some strange oversight, he was not taught Greek in England. He has travelled widely, and this began at an early age. I have mentioned some of his childhood journeys. He has taken several holidays in Europe with some of his cousins. When he went to Australia he flew across the U.S.A. making only two brief stops so that he could hardly be said to have seen anything of that vast land. When he returned from Australia he came by way of Auckland, New Zealand, and after a halt at Tahiti, went on to Mexico. To anyone interested in archaeology Mexico is indeed the land of promise and the prince took the opportunity to visit the famous pyramids of Teotihuacan. Mustered for his delectation by the British Ambassador at a party were some of the most lovely Mexicans but they appeared to arouse no particular interest in the prince.

Not only extensive travel but meeting with important or highly placed persons is the prince's due. Writing of the prince and Princess Anne as far back as 1959, I said: "The royal children are, of course, accustomed to the presence of distinguished visitors as diverse as the King of Iraq, the King of Libya, and Marshal Bulganin and Mr. Khrushchev. To mark the occasion, the King of Libya presented Prince Charles with a splendid Arab saddle made of red velvet and worked with gold and silver. To Princess Anne he gave a golden object called the Hand of Fatima, named after the only child and daughter of Mohammed the Prophet to survive infancy. Marshal Bulganin and Mr. Khrushchev delighted Princess Anne with the gift of a bear cub, Nikki, now one of the attractions of the London Zoo."

When the prince reached Sydney on the way to Timbertop, he was received by Lord Casey, the Governor General, and Mr. Holt, the Prime Minister of Victoria.

Apart from the interruptions caused in his study routine by

these necessary official contacts, there are other more important calls upon the prince's time. When it was decided that he should be invested as Prince of Wales on 1st July 1969, at Caernarvon Castle, it was also decided that he should take a crash course in Welsh at the University of Aberystwyth, lasting one term. Welsh is not an easy language, and those millions who heard the prince speaking in Welsh at his investiture and on other subsequent occasions will realize how hard he must have worked. This, too, in the midst of his university reading. How many young men would like to be compelled to learn a language and to take this just as an extra in the course of their reading for a university honours degree?

The investiture brought Prince Charles to the beginning of his public career. Behind him are the comparatively carefree days of childhood and boyhood. From now on the prince takes his place in assuming the burdens of royalty. The queen has many functions which she cannot delegate even to the Duke of Edinburgh, but she does look to the members of her family to assist her in bringing the royal presence into every part of the national life. While Princess Margaret, Princess Alexandra, the Duke of Gloucester and others take their part, it is naturally to her own children, and particularly to her eventual successor, that the queen must look, as the years pass, for those who will share her task.

This book began with the account of the investiture of Prince Charles's great uncle, the Duke of Windsor. It is fitting that it should close with a description of the prince's own investiture. The 58 years which have passed between 1911 and 1969 have witnessed a revolution in human affairs. The position of Britain has profoundly changed. Instead of being the world's first power and largest empire, she has shrunk to a position in which she can scarcely be described as independent. Yet she still has her ancient monarchy and the ceremony at Caernarvon is an augury that the majority of the British people wish to preserve their throne. The great nations of Europe and Asia have abandoned monarchy. Germany, Italy, Austria and Russia have driven out their dynasties; Turkey and China also. Nor is it only a matter of changing from monarchy to republic. In Russia and China, an ideology, new in theory, but ancient in its tyrannical methods, has gripped great populations and bound them by atheistic and materialistic philosophy never propagated before. Along with harsh and brutal conceptions of socialism within their communities, both Russia and China pursue the imperial aims of their predecessors but with far greater efficiency and power. From the Baltic Sea and Central Europe to the Pacific coast extends the vast Communist empire.

The 58 years since 1911 have wrought a tremendous change in the status of the United States. Before the 1914 war America had hardly entered the sphere of world politics, except for her war with Spain in 1898. Now she is the world's strongest country. At the time of the investiture, America was in the last stages of preparing to put men on the moon. This stupendous feat has been accomplished and everyone must be aware of the nature of the industrial organization which had rendered possible an unprecedented accomplishment. The breaking into another world is a testimony to the advance of science in the last half century.

To turn from these scientific and technological marvels to what may be regarded as a medieval ceremony may seem to some to typify the decadence of Britain. It is not so, Britain will fall into complete collapse only if she continues to a logical conclusion her present renunciation of tradition.

Scientific inventions have had a great impact upon ceremonies like the investiture. When Queen Elizabeth II was crowned in 1953, it was possible for the first time for many millions of her subjects and others who were not, to share in the ceremony. All were impressed, and not least those living in foreign countries. So, too, with the investiture. Instead of relying on written or even broadcast accounts, hundreds of millions were able to see for themselves. It is not too much to say that the eyes of the free world were focused on an ancient castle in a small country which thus achieved a publicity of which it could not otherwise have been the recipient. This fact alone differentiates the investiture of 1969 from its predecessor.

The next great difference between the prince's investiture and that of 1911, lay in the adaptation of the ceremonial and of the prince's clothes to a more sensible style. There is a belief in foreign lands and also among some sections in Britain, that the latter is a land ridden by tradition. According to this view everyone and everything British is fenced in by traditions which resemble the laws of the Medes and Persians in that they may not be changed. Nothing could be further from the truth. Two instances will make this clear. There is supposed to be some sort of ruling that a peer may not be made premier. In fact, 'the century started with a peer in office as premier, and it is only since 1923–24 that the so-called tradition has been made. Again, it used to be a tradition that the Lord Mayor of London on retiring was made a baronet, but this has gone by the board since 1964. Britain is indeed a country where action is fettered at every turn by what is often called red tape; the rules made by officialdom and the restrictions imposed by a vast mass of legislation put out by socialist-minded politicians. This is not tradition, but rather the result of the decline of Britain since 1918. British tradition on the other hand is a living thing which corresponds to the needs of the times. In 1911 the investiture ceremony was revived but it was then given a completely new setting. Previously, up to Stuart times, the Prince of Wales had been invested in the sovereign's palace. Under the Hanoverian rulers with their ignorance of British customs and gross manners, combined with hostility to their heirs, the investiture had been little more than a matter of issuing Letters Patent. Therefore in 1911 not only was the ceremony revived as it had been in the Stuart period but a new form was added to it, by the transference of the ceremony to Caernarvon. In this way a new tradition—that the investiture takes place in Wales—began. There is no slavish adherence, however, and thus the clothes to which the Duke of Windsor so much objected (see page 13) were not *de rigeur* for Prince Charles.

The dress of the prince was the Number One blue (ceremonial) uniform of the Royal Regiment of Wales. Over this he wore a mantle similar to that worn by the Duke of Windsor, but without the train. Gone then were all the fussy details of satin breeches, etc. Three weeks before the investiture on 11th June, the prince, who is Colonel in Chief of the new Royal Regiment of Wales, presented their colours in Cardiff. The regiment has been formed by the amalgamation of the South Wales Borderers and the Welsch Regiment. The prince's uniform included a blue cap with a red band. The collar badges represent the symbols of the two old regiments, the red dragon of the Welsh and the wreath of Immortelles of the Borderers, the latter having been taken in commemoration of a victory over the French.

During the ceremonial the queen invested the prince with (1) the Mantle; (2) the Sword; (3) the Coronet; (4) the Gold Ring which she placed on the third finger of the prince's left hand, and (5) the Gold Rod or Verge. These five emblems were used at the investiture of Henry of Monmouth, later Henry V. Not the same objects, as most English royal insignia were melted down or otherwise disposed of during the rule of Cromwell. The significance of the emblems is, with the Sword, defence; the Rod, authority, and the Ring has the beautiful symbolism that the prince is married to his country of Wales and a father to her children. The Mantle was made for the investiture and was of royal purple silk velvet, trimmed with white ermine and sealskin dots, and adorned with the 18 carat Welsh gold clasp used at the 1911 investiture. The Coronet was specially designed and was a modernized version of the traditional form of coronet, consisting of a circlet bearing alternate crosses and fleurs de lis spanned by a single arch surmounted by an orb and cross. The Coronet was made from 18 carat gold set with diamonds and emeralds, the base is ermine and the cap of state inside is of purple velvet to match the mantle. This is the first coronet or crown made by electroforming, by chemists rather than by jeweller craftsmen beating out sheets of gold. A wax mould of the Coronet was immersed in a plating bath for two and one half days, while the gold was deposited on it. The Coronet was thus made of chemically pure gold and is thinner and half as heavy as if it had been made by traditional methods.

As will be seen in the account of the ceremony, very much greater emphasis was given to the Welsh than in 1911. Of the 4,000 people present, some 3,500 were persons living and working in Wales, a cross section of the Welsh national life. The copy of the ceremonial was printed in both Welsh and English. Welsh brass bands played, and the B.B.C. Welsh orchestra gave a programme of music, with the various Welsh choirs.

At 2 P.M. on 1st July, the royal procession of the queen, the Duke of Edinburgh, the Prince of Wales and other members of the royal family who had come up by overnight train to Caernarvon, were received in the grounds of Ferodo Ltd. Later the carriage procession of the Prince of Wales left the grounds for the Caernarvon Castle. The route was lined by members of the armed forces and the prince's carriage was escorted by a prince's escort of Household Cavalry. The prince had with him in his carriage the Secretary of State for Wales, the Right Honorable George Thomas, and the Equerry to the Prince, Squadron Leader David Checketts. On arrival at the castle the prince's personal banner for Wales (showing the arms of the last native prince) was broken over the Eagle Tower, and a fanfare was sounded from the battlements by the State Trumpeters of the Household Cavalry. After this the prince and his attendants went to the Chamberlain Tower, there to await the summons from the queen.

Then came the queen's procession, saluted by 21 guns fired by a battery of the 22nd Light Air Defence Regiment of the Royal Artillery, and escorted by a Sovereign's Escort of the Household Cavalry. On arrival at the castle, Queen Elizabeth was met by the Constable (her brother-in-law, the Earl of Snowdon, husband of Princess Margaret). He bore the castle key on an oak tray and addressed Her Majesty: 'Madam, I surrender the key of this Castle into Your Majesty's hand.' The queen touched the key and replied: 'Sir, Constable, I return the key of this Castle into your keeping.'

When the queen entered the castle, the Royal Banner in place of that of Prince Charles was broken from the Eagle Tower, while a fanfare was sounded by the State Trumpeters. The queen was conducted to the Dais in the centre of the castle, accompanied by the Great Officers of State, the Constable and the Home Secretary, the Right Honorable James Callaghan.

Having taken her seat on the Dais with the Duke of Edinburgh the queen commanded the Earl Marshal, the Duke of Norfolk, to direct Garter King of Arms to summon the prince. The Garter King then went to the Chamberlain Tower and conveyed the queen's command to the prince. A procession was formed and the prince was conducted to the queen, accompanied by some Welsh peers bearing the insignia with which he was to be invested. By Garter King of Arms the Letters Patent by which the prince was created were delivered to the Lord Great Chamberlain who presented them to the queen. The queen handed the Letters Patent to the Home Secretary, and the Welsh text to the Secretary of State for Wales.

Now the prince accompanied by the peers who supported him, approached the queen, making three separate obeisances to her, and knelt on a cushion before her. The Home Secretary read the Letters Patent in English and the Secretary of State for Wales read the Welsh text. During this reading the queen invested the prince with the insignia of his principality and of the earldom of Chester.

Then came the most moving part of the whole ceremony. The prince kneeling before the queen placed his hands between hers and made declaration: 'I, Charles, Prince of Wales, do become your liege man of life and limb and earthly worship, and faith and truth I will bear unto you to live and die against all manner of folks.'

The queen received the Letters Patent from the Home Secretary, gave them to the prince, and raised him, exchanging with him the Kiss of Fealty. The prince then went to his seat at the queen's right hand. A loyal address to which the prince replied in Welsh, and a religious service then followed. In his speech the prince referred to the famous goon, Harry Seccombe, and raised a laugh; it is well known that the prince greatly enjoys the goon type of humour.

The queen, accompanied by the Duke of Edinburgh, whose part in the ceremonial was that of a spectator, then presented the Prince of Wales to the people of the country at three points (1) Queen Eleanor's Gate, overlooking Castle Square; (2) on the steps outside King's Gate, the main entrance to the castle and (3) the Lower Ward (inside the castle). At each of the three points a fanfare was sounded by trumpeters of the Royal Military School of Music.

On leaving the castle, the royal family witnessed an impressive Royal Air Force fly past. The procession then returned through the streets of Caernarvon to the grounds of Ferodo Ltd Apart from a slight booing at one point and the throwing of a banana skin by some Welsh (possibly Englander) louts, who were promptly dealt with by the police and the magistrates, the crowds showed their accustomed love of the royal family and royal pageantry.

The prince spent the night of 1st July on the Royal Yacht at Holyhead, and on 2nd July began a four-day tour of Wales. The weather during the investiture had been dry, though not sunny, which was a great advantage, nor was the tour marred either by trouble with the elements or with human malcontents. Soviet Radio described the prince's progress as being accompanied by the explosion of bombs and burning cars all along the royal route. This complete fabrication must have been intended for home consumption, since it is well known to all in this country to be untrue.

The prince's progress through Wales lasted from 2nd to 5th July inclusive. He travelled by road, by helicopter and by the Royal Yacht *Britannia*. On 2nd July he started from Llandudno, through the Conway Valley, by Lake Bala to Newport in Montgomeryshire, to New Quay, Cardiganshire and Fishguard. On 3rd July Prince Charles attended a service at St. David's Cathedral, thence travelling by car in Carmarthenshire, and on to Llanelli, Swansea, and Moriston. The 4th July saw him in the mining areas of the south—Merthyr, Ebbw Vale, Brynmawr, Abertillery, Aberberg and Pontypool, ending at Newport. The nights were spent on the yacht. At every stage of the progress, the prince was met by receptions. The 5th July was spent in Cardiff and in the evening he left by train for London.

There for the present we must leave him with the knowledge that for many years to come he will, as Prince of Wales, be headline news. Nothing that he does can lack publicity. Even before the investiture, in March 1969, he had done something which none of his predecessors had ever been called upon to do, in giving an interview to a representative of a news centre. This was the prince's interview with Jack de Manio of the B.B.C., which was broadcast by the corporation. It was an extraordinarily frank and interesting interview, touching in swift review upon the prince's interest in amateur acting, his Welsh descent, the Welsh nationalist extremists, his costume for the investiture, his training at home and school as regards the responsibility which would some day be his, and his experiences in Australia and New Guinea, to which I have referred above.

Prince Charles has also faced the ordeal of a television confrontation with representatives of B.B.C. and I.T.V. (commerical television), in which inevitably the question of his marriage was raised. Because he expressed an opinion, that a princess understood the royal way of life, it started at once a newspaper hunt for eligible princesses. How many people would like to discuss their marriage prospects before an audience of millions?

In conclusion, we may note the action which the prince has announced, that he intends to take with regard to his income from the Duchy of Cornwall. According to a report in the *Times* of 26th August 1969, the prince has decided that on reaching the age of 21 on 14th November 1969, he will give up half the income to which he then becomes entitled. The total revenue from the Duchy of Cornwall estates in 1968 was £217,908. Half of this he has offered to the Consolidated Fund, which means that it will be retained by the Exchequer. This arrangement is subject to review should the prince get married, or if there are other changes in his circumstances. At 21 he is able to have a small household of his own, the expenses being borne out of the revenues of the Duchy.

APPENDIX I

The Duchy of Cornwall

THE Duchy of Cornwall is one of the relics of the ancient demesnes of the Crown which have been left over from the surrender of Crown lands made by George III in return for the sums voted annually in the Civil List.

The possessions of the Duchy of Cornwall comprise lands and buildings in Kennington, mainly industrial and residential, and agricultural land in the counties of Somerset, Dorset, Wiltshire, Devon, Cornwall and the Isles of Scilly, totalling about 14,000 acres; also areas of both foreshore and fundus and mines and minerals in the counties of Devon and Cornwall.

It is not the policy of the Duchy to supply information in regard to its revenue, but it can be stated that no change has been caused by the creation of the new Prince of Wales, nor is likely to be when he comes of age. When the Prince is 21 he will come into the whole of the revenue of the Duchy, but it should not be thought that large sums are being accumulated during his minority. In a report in the *Daily Telegraph* for 24th October 1958 Mr. P. G. T. Kingsley, secretary of the Duchy of Cornwall, said in reference to statements of this nature in the press:

"Some of you [i.e. the tenants of the Duchy] may have read quite recently one such article which told of the income of the Prince of Wales as piling up during the minority, and that it had, in fact, been piling up for twenty years since the last Prince of Wales came to the throne as Edward VIII.

"I have no objection to fairy tales, but one must distinguish between fact and fiction. So I thought it might be of interest in this connection to tell you that, except for a small proportion which is retained for the benefit of the Prince of Wales, dues to the Duchy go to the relief of the Civil List by the Queen."

In Halsbury's *Laws of England*, third edition, vol. 7, there are some thirty pages dealing with various matters about the Duchy of Cornwall. During the minority of the duke the powers and privileges and authorities vested in the duke under the Duchy of Cornwall Management Acts 1863 to 1893 are exercisable by the sovereign as guardian of the duke. There is a council, which is appointed and presided over by Her Majesty whilst the duke remains a minor. This consists at present of:

> H.R.H. The Prince Philip, Duke of Edinburgh.
> The Earl of Radnor (Lord Warden of the Stannaries).
> Sir Edward Peacock (Receiver General).
> The Hon. Charles Russell (Attorney General).
> The Lord Roborough.
> Brig. the Lord Tryon.
> Sir John Carew Pole, Bt.
> Patrick Kingsley, Esq. (Secretary).

The officers appointed for the Duchy are:

> (*a*) Lord Warden of the Stannaries in Cornwall and Devon
> (*b*) Keeper of the Privy Seal
> (*c*) Attorney General
> (*d*) Receiver General.

In addition there are an Auditor, Keeper of the Records, Assistant Secretary, Clerk Accountant, Deputy Receiver, Law Clerk, and Law Steward.

The jurisdiction of the Stannaries Court was abolished in 1896, and it is now vested in the County Court of Cornwall.

The accounts of the Duchy of Cornwall must be submitted annually to the Treasury, and are presented by the Treasury to both Houses of Parliament. The sanction and approval of two or more Treasury Commissioners is required before powers conferred by the Duchy of Cornwall Management Act of 1863 can be exercised.

It may be observed that the lands of the Duchy are not in Wales, and it is not perhaps out of place here to remark on the scant connection of the majority of the Princes of Wales with the country which has been their principality. In this regard it is a curious coincidence that the Duke of Windsor had certain unique connections with the title of Prince of Wales. As far as I can trace there does not seem to have been another Prince of Wales invested and presented to his people as Prince of Wales in Caernarvon Castle between the first Prince (if the old story of his presentation as a baby is to be believed) and that of Edward, Prince of Wales in 1911. Then again, the extensive travels of the Duke of Windsor when he was Prince of Wales took him through tracts of Wales which few of his predecessors had even seen, and when they had seen them it was usually due to the exigencies of war.

In a large work by Edward Parry, written in 1850 under the title *Royal Visits and Progresses to Wales, and the Border Counties of Cheshire, Salop, Hereford and Monmouth, from the first invasion of Julius Caesar, to the friendly visit of Her Most Gracious Majesty Queen Victoria,* every effort has been made to scrape together every case of a royal visit. If we take the author's own definition of the area to be considered as including the counties of the Welsh March, we find:

(i) Edward II was received by the Burgesses of Shrewsbury, went to Flint, and was a refugee in Wales at the close of his reign, when he was captured by Mortimer and the queen.

(ii) Edward III hunted on the border.

(iii) Richard II went to Wales and it was at Conway Castle that he was forced to yield himself to his cousin, Bolingbroke.

(iv) Henry IV and his heir, afterwards Henry V, were in warfare with the Welsh, hardly a royal visit.

(v) Edward, son of Henry VI, wandered in Wales with his mother, Queen Margaret of Anjou, during their distress.

(vi) Edward IV was fond of Shrewsbury, and established the court of the president and council of the Marches of Wales at Ludlow. Here he sent his elder son, Edward, afterwards Edward V, for his education. From there the young king journeyed to London, and his disappearance.

(vii) Henry VII landed at Milford Haven and many Welshmen
joined his standard. Henry VII occasionally visited Wales,
and made progresses there.

(viii) Arthur Prince of Wales, son of Henry VII, took up
residence with his bride at Ludlow.

(ix) Henry VIII was never in Wales but sometimes on the
borders. He consolidated the laws of England and Wales,
so that they form one whole, 1542.

(x) The Princess Mary, daughter of Henry VIII, was early
educated at Ludlow.

(xi) No sovereign visited Wales until in 1617 James I did so.

(xii) Charles I frequently visited Wales and the borders mainly
due to the Civil Wars.

(xiii) Charles II wandered on the borders during his escape
after Worcester but did not visit Wales when he was king.

(xiv) James II visited Ludlow and Shrewsbury. William III
passed through Chester.

(xv) The next Prince of Wales to visit Wales was George
afterwards George IV, who in 1806 went to Shrewsbury and
thence into the nearest part of Wales, where he planted a
tree to commemorate his visit, a practice which has since
developed with formidable proportions. George IV also
made a state visit to Wales. Indeed this much-maligned
monarch was the first sovereign of the House of Hanover to
return to the old practice of English kings, of visiting or
making progresses as it was called, throughout their
dominions. With the advent of modern means of transport
it has been possible for the British sovereign to visit large
areas such as would never have been possible for their
predecessors.

(xvi) William had visited Wales when he was Duke of Clarence
with his brother the Prince of Wales.

(xvii) The Princess Victoria also visited many towns in Wales
before she succeeded to the throne.

These instances, collected over many centuries, show that
the practice of the Princes of Wales in visiting their principality
is largely of modern growth. Many of those princes who did
go to Wales, either when they were Princes of Wales or after

they had succeeded to the throne, did so for reasons which were not connected with healthy interest in the lands they ruled.

The practice of sending the Prince of Wales to Ludlow Castle, which prevailed intermittently over a century, was, like many other good habits of the monarchy and royal family, broken by the arrival of German princes in 1714. The proper habit of royal visits was resumed under George, Prince of Wales, Prince Regent and later George IV. Queen Victoria reproached her son that he seldom, if ever, went near the country whence he derived his title. Edward VIII, on the other hand, visited Wales often, including the Welsh coalfields, at a time when distress of the most acute kind dominated them. He knew his Welsh people at first hand.

APPENDIX II

The Royal Marriages Act, 1772

REFERENCES have been made under the account of the present Prince of Wales to the effect that, unlike other children, he is not free to exercise his choice in matters of profession or vocation, nor again in the matter of marriage. What is the position with regard to royal marriages in Britain?

The governing instrument in the matter, to use legal language, is the statute known as the Royal Marriages Act, 1772. This enactment was made in consequence of the marriage of the then Duke of Cumberland to Mrs. Horton, and of the Duke of Gloucester to Lady Waldegrave. These dukes were the younger brothers of George III. This Act of Parliament lays down the conditions under which members of the Royal Family can contract a valid marriage and is intended to guard against undesirable marriages which might affect the succession to the throne.

1. *The consent of the sovereign is required.*

Halsbury's *Laws of England*, vol. vi, 510, states s.l. of the Act

"No descendant of the body of his late Majesty King George the Second, male or female, under the age of twenty-five years (other than the issue of princesses who have married, o⟨r⟩ may hereafter marry into foreign families), is capable ⟨of⟩ contracting matrimony without the previous consent of th⟨e⟩ Sovereign signified under the Great Seal and declared i⟨n⟩ Council; and every marriage or matrimonial contract of an⟨y⟩ such descendant without such consent first had and obtaine⟨d⟩ is, subject as stated below null and void. If obtained th⟨e⟩ Sovereign's consent is directed to be set out in the licence ar⟨⟩

register of marriage and to be entered in the books of the Privy Council.

"Persons, knowingly and wilfully solemnizing or assisting or being present at a marriage, or at the making of any matrimonial contract forbidden by the Act, are, on conviction, liable to incur the penalties provided by the Statutes of Provisors and Praemunire (these are those of 16 Richard II, c. 5.–1392-3 and of 27 Edward III, stat. l. c. i. –1353)."

2. *Condition under which consent of Sovereign is not required.*

s. 2. of the Act qualifies s.l. as follows:

"Provided always . . . that in case any such descendant of the body of his late Majesty King George the Second, being above the age of twenty-five years, shall persist in his or her resolution to contract a marriage disapproved of, or dissented from, by the King, his heirs or successors: that the such descendant, upon giving notice to the King's Privy Council, which notice is hereby directed to be entered in the books thereof, may at any time from the expiration of twelve calendar months after such notice given to the Privy Council as aforesaid, contract such marriage: and his or her marriage with the person before proposed and rejected, may be duly solemnised, without the previous consent of his Majesty, his heirs or successors: and such marriage shall be good, as if this Act had never been made, unless both Houses of Parliament shall, before the expiration of the said twelve months, expressly declare their disapprobation of such intended marriage."

3. *The Act applies to marriages celebrated abroad.*

This was decided by the House of Lords in the Sussex Peerage case (1844) (Clarke and Finnelly's *Reports of Cases decided in the House of Lords*, vol. xi, pp. 85–154). Soon after the death of H.R.H. the Duke of Sussex (Prince Augustus Frederick, sixth son of George III) in the year 1843, a petition was presented to Her Majesty (i.e. Queen Victoria) by Augustus Frederick D'Este, claiming the honours, dignities and privileges of Duke of Sussex, Earl of Inverness and Baron of Arklow.

The claimant's case rested on a marriage at Rome on 4th April 1793 between Prince Augustus Frederick and Lady Augusta Murray, second daughter of the Earl of Dunmore, the marriage being celebrated by a clergyman of the Church of England according to the rites of that Church. The House of Lords resolved that the claimant had not made out his claim to be Duke of Sussex, etc. Lord Cottenham stated: "... my opinion is formed entirely and exclusively upon the Royal Marriages Act.... I entirely agree in the opinion which has been expressed by the learned Judges, inasmuch as by the construction of the Royal Marriages Act, whether the marriage would be valid by the law of Rome or not, it would not be valid by the law of this country."

Lord Campbell stated: "I have no doubt that it is competent to the British Legislature to pass a law making invalid the marriage of particular British subjects all over the world. I have no doubt that it was the object of that Act of Parliament to invalidate marriages of the descendants of George II, without the consent of the Crown, wherever those marriages might be celebrated."

4. Could the period of twelve months' notice to the Privy Council be reduced and, if so, how?

An Act of Parliament or a section of an Act can only be altered by an Act of Parliament. The law on the subject of royal marriages, like the law on other subjects, is open to revision, and the Royal Marriages Act could be altered to meet the requirements of a particular person.

5. Could a member of the royal family avoid the restrictions on his or her marriage under the Act by renouncing his or her rights of succession to the throne?

There is much misunderstanding on the subject of the renunciation of rights of succession. It is sometimes said that a British princess has renounced her rights of succession on her marriage to a foreign sovereign; e.g. when H.R.H. Princess Victoria married King Alfonso XIII of Spain in 1906, but it fact in such cases no renunciation occurs. The marriage with a Roman Catholic automatically excludes the princess from succession to the throne, under the Act of Settlement, 1700.

Furthermore, a renunciation of rights cannot be valid unless an Act of Parliament is passed to give effect to it. When King Edward VIII executed an instrument of abdication on 10th December 1936, a special Act was still necessary to give effect to the king's declaration of abdication (His Majesty's Declaration of Abdication Act, 1936, s.1; Edward VIII, c. 2), an Act to give effect to His Majesty's declaration of abdication. On the Royal Assent being signified to this Act, the Instrument of Abdication then took effect; Edward VIII ceased to be king, and the Royal Marriages Act of 1772 did not then apply to his former Majesty or to the issue of any marriage which he might contract.

6. *Provision for members of the royal family.*

It is to be presumed that in the event of a marriage without royal approval, followed by a renunciation of rights of succession, the royal personage concerned would cease to be provided for under the Civil List Consolidated Fund (Appropriation) Act. Under this Act provision is made for the sovereign, the sovereign's husband (or wife), or widow, and daughters, annually. When King Edward VIII abdicated he ceased to be provided for under the Act.

There is no case known in which notice has been given to the Privy Council as under s. 2 of the Royal Marriages Act. The affair of the Duke of Windsor is *sui generis*, since he was a sovereign. There have been instances apart from that of the Duke of Sussex, where a marriage has been attempted in defiance of the Act, as we saw in the case of the Prince Regent, later George IV, who went through a form of marriage with Mrs. FitzHerbert. This marriage was null and void under the Act, for the prince did not have royal consent to his marriage; in 1795, therefore, he was able without committing bigamy to marry Princess Caroline of Brunswick-Wolfenbuttel while Mrs. FitzHerbert was still alive.

There are thus no historical parallels for a marriage by a member of the royal family without the consent of the sovereign, and after notice given to the Privy Council. It does not require much imagination to consider that if a member of the royal family were to persist in placing notice of marriage before the Privy Council every effort would be made to persuade that member not to persist in going through with the marriage. If, however, the marriage were eventually celebrated, it seems most probable that renunciation of right of succession would be required since the other party to the marriage would be *prima facie* unacceptable to the sovereign.

BIBLIOGRAPHY

THE INVESTITURE OF THE PRINCE OF WALES.

See *Archaeologia Cambrensis. The Journal of Cambrian Archae-ological Association*, vol. xi, Sixth Series, 1911. This contains "The Investiture of the Prince of Wales", in three articles, by Canon R. H. Morris, and with illustrations. The first article contains a block of the arms of the Prince of Wales, as approved by George V. The second article shows the initial letter of King James I's charter granting the principality of Wales to Prince Henry, and also an illustration of the charter itself. The third article describes the ceremony at Caernarvon, and is well illustrated.

ARMORIAL BEARINGS OF THE PRINCE OF WALES.

A useful study on this side of the subject is given in *Armorial Insignia of the Princes of Wales*, by Guy Cadogan Rothery, 1911.

THE EARLDOM OF CHESTER.

The Complete Peerage, vol. iii, gives a good account of the early changes of this earldom. A good account, enriched with much curious learning of the history of the earldom, is found in John Selden's *Titles of Honour*, the Second Part.

LORDSHIP OF THE ISLES.

The story of the Lords of the Isles is really the tale of the Clan Donald. A good account of this is given in *The Clan Donald*, by I. F. Grant (W. & A. K. Johnston, Ltd., 1952).

OTHER WORKS RELATING TO PRINCES OF WALES.

Royal Visits and Progresses to Wales, and the Border Counties of Chester, Salop, Hereford, and Monmouth, from the first invasion of Julius Caesar, to the friendly visit of Her Most Gracious Majesty

Queen Victoria, by Edward Parry. This is one of those works (written in 1850) which should be carefully preserved. It has a mass of information about it which is unlikely ever to be assembled again, and which certainly will never again be published in such a form. The book is a great tome running to 500 quarto pages. There are numerous mentions of persons who were Princes of Wales. The tenor of the fervid Welsh patriotism may be judged by the fact (on p. 150) that the author speaks of the close of the ancient British Empire, with the death of David, the brother of the last native Prince of Wales. "The death of David closed the sovereignty of the ancient British Empire, which, according to the Cambrian Records, continued from the first coming of Brutus, 1136 before Christ, to 1282 after Christ, a period combining not less than two thousand four hundred and eighteen years." Quite obviously this author was a lover of Geoffrey of Monmouth and would have been horrified at the blasphemies, as he would have thought them, of Sir Thomas Kendrick in doubting the authenticity of the British History.

Dr. Doran: *The Book of the Princes of Wales* (1860). This author also produced the well-known work *Jacobite London*. In all his writings he included many curious details not found elsewhere.

Thomas Sydney: *Heirs Apparent* (Allan & Wingate, 1957). This deals with the Princes of Wales from the time of George I.

E. Thornton Cook: *Kings in the Making. The Princes of Wales* (John Murray, 1931). This traces the Princes of Wales from Edward of Caernarvon, the first, to the Duke of Windsor.

Sir George Arthur: *Seven Heirs Apparent* (Thornton Butterworth, 1937). Here again, as in Sydney's book, we have the princes from the time of George I.

I. Kyrle Fletcher: *The British Court* (Cassell, 1953). Contains interesting details of the Investiture of the Prince of Wales.

HISTORY OF WALES.

The best is by Sir John Edward Lloyd, in two volumes (Longmans, Green & Co., 1948). From the earliest times to the Edwardian Conquest.

THE PRINCES OF WALES

(1)	Edward (Edward II), created Prince of Wales	1301
(2)	Edward the Black Prince, son of Edward III	1343
(3)	Richard (Richard II), son of the Black Prince	1377
(4)	Henry of Monmouth (Henry V)	1399
(5)	Edward of Westminster, son of Henry VI	1454
(6)	Edward of York or of the Sanctuary (Edward V)	1472
(7)	Edward of Middleham, son of Richard III	1483
(8)	Arthur, son of Henry VII	1489
(9)	Henry (Henry VIII), son of Henry VII	1503
(10)	Henry, son of James I	1610
(11)	Charles (Charles I), son of James I	1616
(12)	Charles (Charles II), son of Charles I	1630
(13)	James Francis Edward, "The Old Pretender"	1688
(14)	George Augustus (George II), son of George I	1714
(15)	Frederick Lewis, son of George II	1727
(16)	George William Frederick (George III)	1751
(17)	George Augustus Frederick (George IV)	1762
(18)	Albert Edward (Edward VII)	1841
(19)	George (George V)	1901
(20)	Edward (Edward VIII)	1911
(21)	Charles, Prince of Wales	1958

PRINCES OF WALES

The names of the sovereigns are given in capitals; numbers in brackets denote Princes of Wales

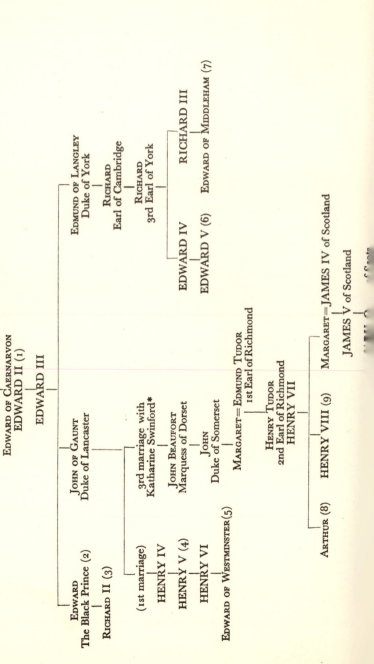

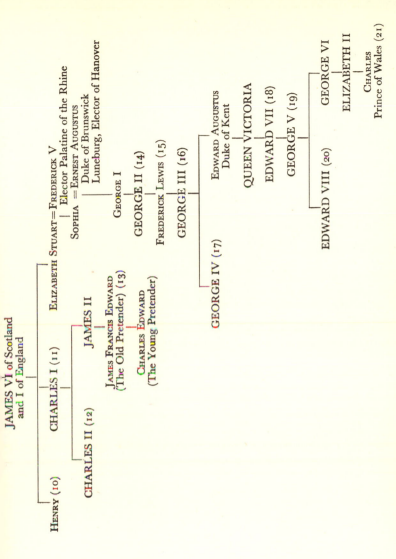

JAMES VI of Scotland
and I of England

HENRY (10)

CHARLES I (11)

ELIZABETH STUART = FREDERICK V
Elector Palatine of the Rhine

SOPHIA = ERNEST AUGUSTUS
Duke of Brunswick
Luneburg, Elector of Hanover

GEORGE I

GEORGE II (14)

FREDERICK LEWIS (15)

GEORGE III (16)

CHARLES II (12)

JAMES II

JAMES FRANCIS EDWARD (13)
(The Old Pretender)

CHARLES EDWARD
(The Young Pretender)

GEORGE IV (17)

EDWARD AUGUSTUS
Duke of Kent

QUEEN VICTORIA

EDWARD VII (18)

GEORGE V (19)

EDWARD VIII (20)

GEORGE VI

ELIZABETH II

CHARLES
Prince of Wales (21)

*The Beaufort children of John of Gaunt and Katharine Swinford were born before the marriage but subsequently legitimised.

INDEX